S0-AET-762

FAITH OF OUR FATHERS

A Bible Commentary for Laymen/Genesis
BY RONALD YOUNGBLOOD

G. Allen Fleece Library
Columbia International University
Columbia, SC 29203

A BIBLE
COMMENTARY
FOR LAYMEN

 **Regal Books** A Division of G/L Publications
Ventura, CA U.S.A.

Other good Regal reading on related subjects:
　　Getz, *Abraham*
　　Getz, *Moses: Moments of Glory, Feet of Clay*
　　LaSor, *Men Who Knew God*
　　Mears, *What the Old Testament Is All About*
　　Ramm, *His Way Out*

The foreign language publishing of all Regal books is under the direction of Gospel Literature International (GLINT). GLINT provides financial and technical help for the adaptation, translation and publishing of books for millions of people worldwide. For information regarding translation, contact: GLINT, P.O. Box 6688, Ventura, California 93006.

All Scripture quotations, unless otherwise noted, are from the *New American Standard Bible* © The Lockman Foundation 1960, 1962, 1963, 1968, 1971. Used by permission.

Copyright © 1976 by Regal Books
All rights reserved

Fourth Printing, 1981

Published by Regal Books
A Division of GL Publications
Ventura, California 93006
Printed in U.S.A.

Library of Congress Catalog Card No. 75-23514
ISBN 0-8307-0370-5

The publishers do not necessarily endorse the entire contents of all publications referred to in this book.

CONTENTS

A Teacher's Manual and a Student Discovery Guide for use with *Faith of Our Fathers* are available from your church supplier.

PREFACE

"The Bible is its own best commentary."

I'm not sure who it was that first made that statement, but it's a good one. The principle it embodies has been of great help to Bible students, commentators, and teachers down through the years. And as I was writing this layman's commentary on Genesis 12—50, I found that statement forcing its way into my thoughts and encouraging me again and again.

In fact, I'm almost ready to reword it as follows:

"The Bible is a better commentary on itself than all other commentaries put together!"

But that would probably be going a little too far. After all, the Bible, despite the fact that its teachings are inexhaustible, is a finite book to the extent that it doesn't tell us everything about everything. So I had to use Bible dictionaries, atlases, histories, commentaries, and other specialized volumes in attempting to explain various details in the stories of the patriarchs.

"The stories of the patriarchs"—what a fascinating study this has been for me! In terms of sheer drama, Genesis 12—50 is one of the most exciting sections in all of Holy Scripture. Written with a flair for suspense and crisis, these chapters of Genesis flow logically from one to another as they tell tales of love and hate, of war and peace, of generosity and selfishness, of violence and gentleness—but, most of all, of faith.

Yes, of faith—because while the stories of the patriarchs sweep across the entire spectrum of human emotion and experience, their main objective, I believe, is to show how men and women who possessed profound faith in God overcame obstacles that would have been the despair or death of lesser people.

So, my purpose in writing this book has been twofold. I've tried to explain Genesis 12–50, sometimes by retelling the patriarchal stories but always by showing the interlocking relationships between the various parts of what I believe to be a unified account. And I've tried to do so first and foremost by making use of related passages of Scripture, whether from within Genesis itself or from elsewhere in the Old Testament or, last but by no means least, from the New Testament.

The perceptive reader will detect that quite a bit of what the following pages contain is not original with me. I owe a great debt of gratitude to all from whom I have learned in the past as well as to all from whom I continue to learn, some of whose works are listed in the bibliography at the end of the book. Grateful appreciation is also due to Nikki Daniels, who typed the final manuscript in the midst of an already crowded schedule.

Most of all, however, I wish to give my heartfelt thanks to my wife Carolyn and our teenagers, Glenn and Wendy. Writing a book leaves a man less time to tend to his "patriarchal" duties at home, and my family filled in for me beautifully and uncomplainingly.

Come to think of it, things have never been in better shape around the house than they are right now!

Ronald Youngblood

1

THE BEGINNING:
God's Covenant People

What are we trying to accomplish in this book?

Our main purpose is to investigate the beginnings, the historical beginnings, of our Christian faith. Genesis, after all, is the book of beginnings. It tells us about the beginning of the universe, of the world, of plant life, of animal life, of human life, of sin, etc. But most of all it tells us about the beginning of religion, about the beginning of our faith.

Who, then, founded our faith?

Some might answer, "The apostle Paul, of course. After all, he took the teachings of Jesus and combined them into a comprehensive theology that tells us how we can be reconciled to God and properly related to each other."

But another might say, "No, actually we have to go back to Jesus Christ Himself as the founder of our faith. In fact, Hebrews 12:2 calls Him the pioneer, the author, of our faith, so that would seem to settle the matter."

Still another might argue, "Wait a minute. Jesus Himself would have been the first to admit that much of what He said was not new. Many of the things Jesus taught are found in the Old Testament, the only Bible He knew. One of His favorite books was Deuteronomy, and He quoted often from its pages. He placed Moses' writings on a par with His own words (John 5:46, 47), so we should probably trace the origins of our faith all the way back to Moses!"

Now each of these three answers is a good answer, and each contains a certain measure of truth in it. But when all is said and done, we would do well to observe that the Bible itself traces our faith back to a period earlier than that of Paul or of Jesus or even of Moses—it traces our faith to the period of the patriarchs, the period of Abraham, Isaac and Jacob.

The most intimate, personal name of God during the Old Testament period was Yahweh, translated in some modern English versions as "the LORD" (spelled with all capital letters). When the Hebrew people were at their spiritual best, they placed their complete faith and trust in "the LORD, the God of their fathers, the God of Abraham, the God of Isaac, and the God of Jacob" (Exod. 4:5.) "The LORD" was the name of the God of the patriarchs, who often enjoyed intimate spiritual fellowship with Him.

The unexcelled leader of the patriarchs was Abraham, who became the prototype of the man of faith, "the father of all who believe" (Rom. 4:11). We who are Christians "are of the faith of Abraham" (4:16); we, in effect, share his faith.

Needless to say, people worshiped the one true God long before Abraham's time (Gen. 4:26). But it is nevertheless true that the basic covenant promises of God were first given to Abraham, the spiritual father of the Hebrew people. In fact, Abraham was the first person in the Bible to be called a "Hebrew" (14:13). And it was through Abraham's Hebrew descendants that God's promises were transmitted to the nation of Jacob (later renamed Israel), the tribe of Judah, and the family of David, from which eventually came our Lord Jesus Christ, the supreme object of our faith. Significantly, it is to Abraham that the New Testament takes us back in its very first verse: "The book of the genealogy of Jesus Christ, the son of David, the son of Abraham" (Matt. 1:1).

The Biblical Source Material—Genesis 11:27—50:26

The book of Genesis is divided into two unequal halves: 1:1—

7

11:26 and 11:27—50:26. Each half has five sections, and each section is introduced by the phrase, "These are the generations of . . . ," or its equivalent. The first half of Genesis, sometimes called the "Primeval History," exhibits that phrase at 2:4; 5:1; 6:9; 10:1 and 11:10 (the creation account of 1:1—2:3 forms the introduction to the book as a whole).

The second half of Genesis, sometimes called the "Patriarchal History," exhibits the characteristic phrase at the beginning of the stories dealing mainly with Abraham (11:27—25:11), Ishmael (25:12-18), Jacob (25:19—35:29), Esau (36:1—37:1) and Joseph (37:2—50:26). Terah (Abraham's father), Ishmael, Esau and even Isaac do not receive much attention in the narrative.

The writer is concerned primarily with the careers of Abraham, Jacob and Joseph, so he gives each of them an average of ten or more chapters: More than 60 percent of the book of Genesis deals with the lives of these three men! We, then, will also concentrate our attention on the careers of these men, because we want to observe the law of proportion when reading and studying our Bibles.

The Historical Setting

Were the patriarchs merely wandering shepherds, primitive nomads in a world of very little culture and sophistication? That's what people used to think. But we now know, due to research carried on over the past 150 years or so, that the patriarchs lived at some time during what archaeologists call the Middle Bronze Age (c. 2100 to c. 1550 B. C.), a period of high cultural achievement.

Mesopotamia

Genesis 11:27—38:30 is a section that stresses the Mesopotamian origins of and influences on the patriarchs. During most of the patriarchal period, the First Dynasty of Babylon (c. 1894 to c. 1595 B. C.)[1] held sway in Mesopotamia. Roughly Syria and Iraq today, *Mesopotamia* was the name given to the territory by ancient Greek writers because it was the land "between the (Euphrates and Tigris) rivers."

In many respects, the First Dynasty of Babylon represented a kind of Golden Age in the history of Mesopotamia. It was the time that its people looked back to fondly as the "good old days" when they thought about their past history. It included the reign of the famous King Hammurabi (c. 1792 to c. 1750 B. C.), whose code of laws is justly the most enduring monument to his greatness. So powerful and so cultured was Mesopotamia during this period that its language, Akkadian, became the *lingua franca*, the language of diplomacy, throughout the then-known civilized world. Mesopotamian society became unified and stabilized; science and literature assumed characteristic forms that would last for centuries; religion became canonized and took on new prominence.

Such was the age of the patriarchs in ancient Mesopotamia!

Egypt

Genesis 39—50 portrays the migration of the patriarchs to Egypt and their settlement in that land. There, also, people were enjoying a kind of Golden Age during most of the patriarchal period. The Egyptian Middle Kingdom era (Dynasty XII), which lasted from 1991 to 1786 B. C., represents in many respects the highwater mark of ancient Egypt's art and literature, of her commercial and political power.

People looked back fondly to the Middle Kingdom period as the "good old days" in their past history. The capital of Egypt was the beautiful city of Thebes on the upper Nile, there was a flourishing copper and turquoise mining industry deep in the interior of the Sinai peninsula, and the Egyptians were able to exert control over much of Syria and Palestine. They erected magnificent buildings, fashioned exquisite jewelry and wrote literary epics of lasting impact. Among the greatest of these was the *Tale of Sinuhe,* a story describing the voluntary exile of an Egyptian nobleman and incidentally demonstrating the ease of travel and communication between Egypt and Palestine at the time of the Middle Kingdom.

During this period, Egyptian science also reached its highwater mark. So careful were the observations made by Egypt's astronomers and so exact was their record-keeping that 1991 B. C., the first year of Dynasty XII, is also the earliest precise year-date in human history. And Egypt's best-known and most enduring monuments, the pyramids in the Gizeh group near modern Cairo, had already been built 500 years before the Twelfth Dynasty began!

Such was the age of the patriarchs in ancient Egypt!

The Hittites

Sprinkled throughout Genesis 11:27—50:26 are numerous references to the Hittites, the sons of Heth (Gen. 10:15). Now recognized as the third great Near Eastern empire of ancient times, the Hittites flourished in Asia Minor (modern Turkey) from c. 1800 to c. 1200 B. C. While the word "Hittite" in the Old Testament refers to several different cultures (see Gen. 23 and 2 Sam. 11 for two of them), the early Hittites of the patriarchal period were instrumental in the mass importation of the horse into Asia Minor. They also used chariots from the beginning of their history, and until the onset of the Iron Age (c. 1200 B. C.) they had a virtual monopoly on iron-smelting techniques, which made them fearsome warriors.

So during the early years of Hittite history, the biblical patriarchs were trying to make their way in a period of great progress!

The Dates

James Ussher, who was Archbishop of Armagh in northern Ireland in the seventeenth century, calculated the date of Abraham's birth (Gen. 11:26) as 1996 B. C. and the date of Joseph's entrance into Egypt (37:36) as 1728 B. C. Although Ussher's calculations sometimes resulted in other dates that are wide of the mark, in this case he seems to have been remarkably accurate, even considering the Old Testament evidence as we understand it today. So although we can't establish early Old Testament chronology simply through dead reckoning, and even though other chronological outlines for the patriarchal period are possible, we can't go far wrong if we round off Ussher's dates and assume that the period of the patriarchs lasted from c. 1990 to c. 1720 B. C.[2]

The Patriarchs Themselves

There were, of course, more than three patriarchs. But when we think of the patriarchs we normally think only of Abraham,

Isaac and Jacob (as, for example, in Exod. 4:5 or Matt. 8:11). In a passage like Acts 7:9, however, the term "patriarchs" is used in a wider sense, referring to the brothers of Joseph. Zion National Park in the state of Utah boasts three impressively high rock formations known as "The Three Patriarchs" and named individually after Abraham, Isaac and Jacob, again demonstrating the narrower use of the term. The names of some of the biblical patriarchs have been found in nonbiblical documents contemporary with the patriarchal period. But more about this later.

What "Patriarch" Means

The word "patriarch" means "father who rules." It refers to the fact that in the culture of those times the father was the undisputed head of the family and the clan. At the risk of being called a male chauvinist, I strongly affirm my support of that arrangement, which I believe to be thoroughly biblical (see especially Eph. 5:21—6:4). Generally speaking, societies in which the father is the head of the home experience very little juvenile delinquency. This has been traditionally the case in countries as different as China and Italy.

Now this understanding of family relationships does not relieve the mother of her obligation to share in the difficult task of raising the children in the nurture and admonition of the Lord. It simply emphasizes the fact that the final responsibility and burden for that task rest squarely on the shoulders of the father.

That's the way it was in patriarchal times, and that's the way it ought to be today.

Their Original Homeland

One of my students proposed several years ago, only half seriously, that the story of Abraham's life could be entitled "From Ur to Eternity." Actually that's not a bad title, since the patriarchs originally came from Ur of the Chaldeans in Mesopotamia.

We know that their forefathers worshiped other gods (Josh. 24:2) and were no doubt idolaters, since the patron deity of Ur was a moon-god. It may well be that Terah's decision to leave Ur and migrate westward was influenced by the Elamite invasion of

11

Ur c. 1950 B. C. or slightly earlier (an Elamite king is mentioned in Gen. 14:1). But even though Terah had apparently intended to go directly to Canaan from Ur, he and his family stopped off for a while in Haran (11:31), where he died (11:32). God told Abraham to move on to Canaan. The call of God and Abraham's obedient response of believing faith to that call are basic to biblical religion.

Their Occupations

How did Terah and his sons earn their living?

The late W. F. Albright, dean of American archaeologists and a brilliant Old Testament scholar, developed the tantalizing idea that the patriarchs were basically donkey caravanners who owned herds of donkeys utilized to transport goods from one place to another.[3] These caravanners would have served the same purpose in ancient times that our modern trucking industry does now. If Albright is correct, the patriarchs would have been semi-nomads who confined their travels to the settled land and its fringes, the "Fertile Crescent," which stretched in an enormous arc from the Persian Gulf northwestward up the Tigris-Euphrates river valley to the Haran region and then southwestward into the heartland of Palestine. This would have made it easy for them to pull up stakes and leave Ur at almost any time.

The fact that they are represented in Genesis as herdsmen would then simply indicate what their occupation was between business trips. When they weren't on the road with their donkey caravans, they were home on the range tending their flocks!

Their Customs

When we read the Genesis narrative, many of the patriarchal customs seem rather strange to us, and a few of them actually shock us. But we need to remember two basic facts in this connection: (1) The customs that seem strange to us do so because they were Eastern customs and did not develop from the thought patterns that are characteristic of us Westerners. We must continually remind ourselves that the patriarchs lived thousands of years ago and thousands of miles from where we are here in the west. (2) The customs that shock us, although they were prevalent in the ancient Near East, generally were not condoned by God. The Hebrew people, when they indulged in any of these, invariably suffered untold grief, as we shall see.

Archaeological Insights

Archaeology has cast such a flood of light on the ancient Near East that in some respects we know more about patriarchal Babylonian villages in Mesopotamia than we do about eighteenth-century American colonial villages! There are literally hundreds of thousands of ancient documents, clay tablets, written in Akkadian and other languages, giving us detailed descriptions of life in those early days. Here are a few examples:

The Mari Letters

Thousands of clay letters (or tablets)—excavated by the French beginning in 1933 at the ancient Amorite city of Mari on the Euphrates River—illustrate the freedom of travel that existed between various parts of the Amorite world in the eighteenth century B. C. In them we learn also that the personal names of the patriarchs were typical of that time. Names similar to those of Abraham, Jacob, Job and others are found frequently in the letters.

Ur of the Chaldeans

Today Ur is little more than a camel stop in the desert. A number of years ago, a visitor stayed overnight in the small hotel there and wrote these words in the guest register: "No wonder Abraham left Ur!" And underneath that phrase, written by another traveler, are these words: "Even Job would have!"

But those negative evaluations of Ur do not take into account the British excavations conducted at the site of Ur from 1922 to 1934. Sir Leonard Woolley's expedition uncovered, among other things, the royal death pit at Ur and found gold jewelry, a gold helmet, a gold crown worn by the queen of the city back in those days, and many other items reflecting the fabulous wealth of ancient Ur. In fact, Ur was at the height of its prosperity from c. 2060 to c. 1950 B. C. or a bit earlier, at just about the time Abraham was living there. So it really cost Abraham something to leave Ur! God didn't call him to leave a dirty little town; He called him to leave a cultured and sophisticated city.

Soon after Ur's destruction by the Elamites, a Sumerian lamentation was composed. It reminds us somewhat of the Lamentations of Jeremiah that were written to mourn the destruction of Jerusalem at the hands of Nebuchadnezzar in 586 B. C.

Haran and Nahor

Haran was a flourishing city in the nineteenth and eighteenth centuries B. C. (the late patriarchal period). It is mentioned frequently in ancient cuneiform sources. During the days of Hammurabi, it was ruled by an Amorite prince. The word *har(r)án* means "crossroads" or "caravan" in Akkadian, giving some support to Albright's theory that the patriarchs were donkey caravanners.

As for the city of Nahor (mentioned as the home of Rebekah in Gen. 24:10), it is referred to in the Mari letters (as well as in later Assyrian records of the seventh century B. C.) as being located in the Haran district. Nahor, like Mari, was ruled by an Amorite prince in the eighteenth century B. C. It may well be that Abraham himself was an Amorite.

The Nuzi Tablets

Initially discovered in 1925 near Kirkuk on a branch of the Tigris River, these documents, though dated in the fifteenth century B. C., throw a great deal of light on patriarchal customs. (Customs generally linger on for generations in that part of the world.) The people of Nuzi were basically non-Semitic Hurrians (the Horites of the Bible). Contract documents found at Nuzi illustrate, among other matters, the following:

A. The obligation of a wife to furnish her husband with sons, even through his cohabitation with a servant girl, if necessary (see Gen. 16:2-4);

B. The importance and salability of the birthright (see 25:29-34);

C. The inheritance rights of an adopted slave when there are no sons in the family (see 15:1-4);

D. Strictures against expelling a servant girl and her child (see 21:10,11);

E. The validity of the deathbed bequest (see 49:28-33).[4]

These are a few of the strange and shocking customs we mentioned earlier, and as we proceed through the Genesis stories of the patriarchs we will make further comments about their significance.

Beni Hasan

Moving now from Mesopotamia to Egypt, we observe that a scene painted on the wall of a tomb at Beni Hasan (the tomb is dated c. 1892 B.C.) pictures 37 Asians bringing gifts to an Egyptian nobleman. The painting is very important because it shows what Asians looked like during the patriarchal period. The men wore knee-length skirts and sandals, while the women wore long dresses and shoes that covered the entire foot. Some of the travelers are portrayed as smiths and musicians, reminding us of Genesis 4:21, 22. The gifts and other items are being carried on the backs of donkeys. We recall that Abraham made a trip down into Egypt during a time of famine in Canaan.

The 'apirū

One final archaeological note: ever since the discovery in 1887 at Tell el-Amarna in Middle Egypt of the now-famous Amarna letters, which mention bands of soldiers of fortune called *habirū* (or, more precisely, *'apirū*), attempts have been made to connect the term *'apiru* (plural *'apirū*) with the term "Hebrew" and to equate the invasion of Canaan under Joshua with the intermittent raids of the *'apirū* during the fourteenth century B. C. Such attempts have met with limited success because, while certain similarities between the two groups do exist, certain basic differences are likewise apparent. Also, it is not certain that the late fifteenth or early fourteenth century B. C. is the time when the conquest of Canaan took place.

At any rate, *'apirū* are mentioned from the nineteenth to the twelfth centuries B. C. all the way from Egypt in the west to Mesopotamia in the east and in Egyptian, Canaanite and Akkadian historical sources. A consensus seems to be developing that, in a limited sense at least, the terms *'apiru* and "Hebrew" are equivalent but that *'apiru* is the broader term. To state it somewhat differently, while not all *'apirū* were Hebrews, all Hebrews were originally *'apirū*.[5]

Whether this consensus will hold only time will tell. In any event, "Hebrew" in the Old Testament was an ethnic term, apparently denoting descent from Eber who, according to the table of nations in Genesis 10, was a great-grandson of Shem, Noah's son (Gen. 10:21-24). By contrast, 'apirū was a term applied to various ethnic groups who had in common only an inferior social status. By and large, the life-style of the patriarchs sets them several notches above that of the ordinary 'apirū, who usually lacked both roots and resources. So we can't simply say that the 'apirū and the Hebrews were exactly the same people and let it go at that.

And if it should turn out that the patriarchs were in fact 'apirū, they were 'apirū with a flair for life and a genuine consciousness of God's personal presence.

Footnotes

1. For the most part, the dates given in this chapter are those used by W. W. Hallo and W. K. Simpson in their brief history of ancient Mesopotamia and Egypt entitled *The Ancient Near East: A History* (New York: Harcourt Brace Jovanovich, Inc., 1971).

2. See also K. A. Kitchen and T. C. Mitchell in J. D. Douglas, ed., *New Bible Dictionary* (Grand Rapids: Wm. B. Eerdmans Publishing Co., 1962), pp. 213, 214, 218.

3. See conveniently W. F. Albright, *Yahweh and the Gods of Canaan* (Garden City: Doubleday & Company, Inc., 1968), pp. 64-73.

4. See the useful summary by C. H. Gordon in D. N. Freedman and E. F. Campbell, Jr., editors, *The Biblical Archaeologist Reader, 2* (Garden City: Doubleday Anchor, 1964), pp. 21-33.

5. See Albright, *Yahweh and the Gods of Canaan*, pp. 73-91.

2

ABRAM:

His Land
Genesis 11:27—14:24

The real hero of the book of Genesis is, of course, God Himself, the God who acts in vigorous and marvelous ways on behalf of His people.

But, humanly speaking, the hero of our story is Abram. (We must get used to calling him "Abram" until we reach Gen. 17:5, where he is renamed "Abraham.") He was the forefather of the other patriarchs.

The patriarchs as wanderers, whether donkey caravanners or shepherds or both, is a common biblical theme. Deuteronomy 26:5 begins a beautiful creedal statement that calls one of the patriarchs "a wandering Aramean." Psalm 105:12-15 is part of a poem that refers to the patriarchs as "strangers" who "wandered about from nation to nation."

Because the patriarchs were wanderers in a foreign land, it is understandable that they would long for a land of their own. And because God is a loving God, it is understandable that He would promise to give it to them.

These early chapters of the patriarchal story in Genesis focus their attention on God's promise of a land to Abram and his descendants.

Abram's Call—11:27—12:3

First of all, we receive a formal introduction to Abram's family. His father's name was Terah, he had two brothers named Nahor and Haran, and he had a nephew named Lot (11:27). His wife's name was Sarai, and we are told that Sarai was sterile, unable to bear children (11:29, 30).

Terah decided to make a trip to Canaan and to take Abram, Sarai and Lot along with him (11:31). Was it a business trip? Were the patriarchs fleeing from the Elamites, who were planning to conquer Ur at about this time? We don't know why Terah made his decision, but whatever the reasons, God used that decision for His own redemptive purposes.

Halfway to Canaan they stopped at Haran (spelled differently, in Hebrew, from the name of Abraham's brother). Like Ur, Haran was another place where the moon-god was worshiped. Since Terah was doubtless an idolater (Josh. 24:2), he probably felt comfortable living in Haran and apparently had neither the strength nor the will to continue the journey to Canaan. So there the family stayed until Terah died (Gen. 11:32). And there also God confirmed His choice of Abram as a man who was to do His bidding.

Sometimes God issues a call to an individual more than once. This seems to have been the case with Abram, because according to Stephen's speech in Acts 7:2 God had already appeared to him "in Mesopotamia, before he lived in Haran." And now God was calling him once again (Gen. 12:1). He was saying to him, in effect, "I want you to leave Ur, to leave Haran, to leave everything behind, and to follow Me!" And so, "by faith," that's exactly what Abram did; he "went out, not knowing where he was going" (Heb. 11:8).

Genesis 20:7 tells us that Abram was a prophet. The word "prophet" means literally a "called one," a person who has been called by God to do God's bidding. Working for God, doing God's will, is a "calling," a vocation, not a profession. We don't choose to work for Him; rather, He chooses us to do His work—and it's always because of His grace, not because of any merit or ability of our own. Whenever we do His work in accord with His will, whether part-time or full-time, it is His idea and His choice, not ours.

Abram's call (Gen. 12:1-3) contained a sevenfold promise: land ("the land which I will show you"), descendants ("a great nation"), blessedness ("I will bless you"), fame ("and make your name great"), opportunity for service ("you shall be a blessing"), protection ("I will bless those who bless you, and the one who curses you I will curse") and universal influence ("in you all the families of the earth shall be blessed").

A proper understanding of Abram's call is basic for a proper understanding of biblical religion generally. One or more elements of the call were repeated and reaffirmed to Abram in Genesis 12:7; 15:5-21; 17:4-8; 18:18,19; 22:17,18; to Isaac in 26:2-4; to Jacob in 28:13-15; 35:11,12; 46:3; to Moses in Exodus 3:6-8; 6:2-8, etc.

As Christians, we should be most interested in the seventh promise in Abram's call. Abram's descendants are understood in both a physical and a spiritual sense in the New Testament. In Acts 3:25, Peter referred to the seventh promise in his great temple sermon and related it to his Jewish listeners (see Acts 3:12), to Abram's physical descendants. But in Galatians 3:8, Paul quoted the seventh promise and related it to his Gentile listeners, to Abram's spiritual descendants. If we are Gentile Christians, Paul says, we are Abram's spiritual brothers and sisters; we share Abram's faith and heritage!

From Haran to Canaan to Egypt to Canaan—12:4-20

The title of this brief section underscores for us the fact that the patriarchs were wanderers. Look where Abram went in the space of just 17 verses!

Abram's response to God's call was both noteworthy and praiseworthy. He was characterized by prompt obedience. There was no hesitation, no beating around the bush; when God asked Abram to do something, he did it right away. And this characteristic of obedient promptness followed him throughout his life (see 17:23; 21:14; and, supremely, 22:3).

So, when the Lord told Abram to "go" (12:1), he simply packed his bags and "went" (12:4)—at the age of 75 years! He was starting out on a new venture 10 years beyond modern retirement age—but according to Genesis 25:7 he would live for yet another century! Since he would live to be 175 years old, at 75 he was still relatively young—and maybe that's the way he felt. His father Terah, after all, had died at the age of 205 (11:32).

How are we to understand these references to the longevity of the patriarchs? Did they really live to such advanced ages? Many different answers have been given to this question, but we will confine ourselves to those that seem most probable.

1. *The numbers are to be understood literally.* Perhaps people in those days lived at a slower pace; they did a hard day's work each day, got a good night's rest each night, were not pressured by the high-powered tensions of modern life and ate natural (unprocessed and, therefore, unpolluted) foods. Tribespeople in our own time who follow such a regimen often live unusually long lives. For example, people live well over 100 among the Hunzukuts of north central Pakistan[1] and in certain sections of the Soviet Union.

On September 2, 1973, Shirali Muslimov of the village of Barzavu in the Soviet Caucasus is said to have died at the age of 168![2] However, many researchers doubt this and similar reports, which are based on hearsay rather than any kind of documentary evidence; "no man or woman with a verifiable birth record is known to have lived longer than 113 years."[3] Such doubts should not necessarily cause us to deny the possibility of genuinely unusual longevity among the patriarchs, since unknown factors may have been working to help them live to greatly advanced ages.

2. *Some of the numbers, at least, are to be understood figuratively.* Joseph, for example, is said to have died in Egypt at the age of 110 (Gen. 50:26). Now we know from ancient Egyptian records that 110 years was considered to be the ideal lifespan[4] and that the number 110 in such cases is therefore usually to be understood qualitatively rather than quantitatively. The lifespans of other patriarchs and their wives—127 years (23:1), 137 (25:17), 147 (47:28), 180 (35:28)—could also be similarly evaluated and interpreted, although we have very little evidence today that would enable us to do so confidently.

3. *The patriarchs were special people whom God preserved in special ways for special purposes, and their lifespans should not be judged by normal ancient or modern standards.* If other ordinary people, then or now, have not lived to such advanced ages, that

should not bother us, because the biblical patriarchs were not ordinary people. God's protecting hand was over their lives, and He had promised Abram, for example, that he would be buried "at a good old age" (15:15).

Each of these three widely-held answers has merit—and they are not necessarily mutually exclusive. Perhaps some of the figures are quantitative and others qualitative. But whatever the ultimate answer to the question of patriarchal longevity, the Old Testament clearly wants us to understand that life itself is a gift of God and that long life, in the case of the patriarchs, was a mark of God's blessing and gracious love.

And now, back to our story. Abram, Sarai and Lot set out from Haran in the northern Mesopotamian river valley. They headed southward and probably passed through Damascus where Abram acquired the services of his servant Eliezer (see 15:2). They stopped also at the sanctuary at Shechem in central Canaan, and there the Lord appeared to Abram and confirmed to him the promise of land that he would eventually receive (12:7). Abram expressed his gratitude by worshiping the Lord and building an altar to Him (see also 12:8). He often built altars in places where he had unusually intense spiritual experiences (13:18; 22:9). When God does great things for us today, we too should thank Him in similarly sacrificial and worshipful ways.

Abram and his party then continued on past Bethel and Ai toward the Negev (12:9), the wasteland area south of Beersheba. At some time during their trip famine struck, so when they ran out of provisions they went down to Egypt to stay until the famine was over.

Abram didn't want to die of hunger, but neither did he want to lose his life because of Sarai's beauty. He knew that when they arrived in Egypt the pharaoh's men would see how beautiful Sarai was. Thinking Abram was her husband, the men would kill him and make Sarai just another concubine in the pharaoh's harem.

Sarai's beauty is described only briefly in Genesis 12:11 and 12:14, but it is described in great detail in the so-called *Genesis Apocryphon*, one of the Dead Sea scrolls. Ancient Jewish tradition obviously remembered Sarai as being an unusually beautiful woman, and rightly so. We can therefore understand

Abram's concern to save his own skin as he, Sarai, and Lot approached the borders of Egypt!

Suddenly, he had an idea: he told Sarai to claim she was his sister. At best, this was only a half-truth—since she was only his half-sister (20:12)! So Abram shaved the truth a bit to get out of his predicament.

Now whatever one might think about the morality of the ancient Egyptians, a major principle of their ethics was what they called *maat*, which included a strong emphasis on truth as opposed to falsehood.[5] In other words, the Egyptians had no patience with liars. An incongruous scene, then, is unfolding before us—a man of God telling a "white" lie to a pagan ruler! When the pharaoh later confronted Abram with that lie and its implications, Abram must have felt very small indeed.

But before that happened, the Lord afflicted the pharaoh's household with dreadful diseases to keep Sarai from becoming a concubine in his harem. The pharaoh rightly interpreted the affliction as God's way of punishing him for something evil that he had done, and he eventually figured out that Sarai was Abram's wife. As soon as the lie was discovered, the pharaoh reprimanded Abram and then deported him and the other members of his party. It must have been an embarrassing scene, but unfortunately Abram didn't learn the lesson from it that he should have, as we shall see in Genesis 20.

Settling Down—13:1-18

After being chased out of Egypt by the pharaoh, Abram, Sarai and Lot retraced their steps back through the Negev, back to Bethel and Ai. There Abram again called on the Lord's name (13:4), as he had done earlier (12:8). When we are caught in a lie, or when some other moral or spiritual problem plagues us, we should go back to the place where we met God. There we can beg forgiveness and reaffirm our faith, just as Abram did.

Lot tagged along behind Abram (13:1; 13:5), as he had done before (12:4). But now he begins to assume a more important role in the story. He and Abram had both become wealthy, and their wealth was measured primarily in terms of cattle (12:16; 13:2; 13:5). Camels are mentioned among their animals (12:16), and many scholars consider such references in the patriarchal narrative anachronistic, claiming that camels were not domesticated until a much later period. Careful research has shown, however, that some domestication of the camel did in fact take place during the period of the patriarchs.[6]

Lot's and Abram's herds continued to grow, and pastureland for them became more and more scarce. As often happens in such cases (see 36:7), the land couldn't support the herds of both men. Soon their herdsmen began to quarrel with each other, trying to gain for their flocks the best pastureland and the best water holes (see also 26:20). And to make matters worse, we are told that Canaanites and Perizzites were living in the same area (13:7), and presumably they would need grazing land for their own animals also.

Abram realized that something had to be done quickly. One of the characteristics that made him a great man was his generosity, and it is revealed nowhere more clearly than here. He gave his nephew Lot the choice of the available land.

Lot, a young man with his whole life still before him, perhaps decided that it was only logical for him to choose the best land. After all his uncle Abram was getting along in years and wouldn't need good grazing land for his flocks much longer anyhow. But whatever his reasons, Lot chose the well-watered Jordan valley. In so doing, he took the *first* of seven downward steps that we shall trace—seven downward steps that would lead to his spiritual destruction. He chose that valley "for himself" (13:11); he made a selfish choice. Selfishness is often the first downward step in a person's spiritual experience. In Lot's case, it formed quite a contrast to Abram's generosity.

Lot's *second* downward step was that he moved his tents in the direction of Sodom (13:12). By doing that, he was putting himself in a precarious spiritual position, because Sodom had already gained a reputation for its wickedness (13:13).

We noted that Lot's selfishness was in contrast to Abram's generosity. Let's observe two other contrasts between Lot and Abram in Genesis 13.

Lot "lifted up his eyes" (13:10) and coveted the well-watered Jordan valley. The Lord said to Abram, "Lift up your eyes" (13:14), and then He showed him the land that would eventually belong to him and his descendants. (Hundreds of years later, the

Lord would show Moses the same land on the eve of its conquest; see Deut. 34:1-4.) Lot lifted up his own eyes and caved in before the pressures of his own desire; Abram lifted up his eyes at God's command and was blessed because of his submissive obedience.

Lot "moved his tents" (13:12) in the direction of a wicked city. Abram "moved his tent" (13:18) in the direction of Hebron, and there he built an altar to worship the Lord. Lot moved for his own convenience and comfort; Abram moved for spiritual reasons.

Lifting up eyes and moving tents are neither good nor bad in themselves. They are both neutral activities. But in Genesis 13 the results of those actions were contrasting, because Lot stubbornly followed his own will while Abram tried only to do the will of God.

The Battle of the Kings—14:1-24

If we could identify the kings mentioned in Genesis 14 with any degree of certainty, we could then date the patriarchs more precisely than we were able to do back in chapter one. But all we can say about these kings is that their names are typical of royal names known from ancient Akkadian, Hittite and other inscriptions. At one time Amraphel (14:1) was equated with the great Babylonian king Hammurabi, but that attempted identification has now been given up by most scholars.

Some of the place-names and peoples mentioned in Genesis 14 are relatively unknown, while others are more familiar. Elam (14:1) was the nation located some distance east of Ur. Sodom and Gomorrah (14:2) were the infamous towns situated somewhere near the southern end of the Dead Sea, here called the "Salt Sea" (14:3) because of its high chemical content. The Horites (14:6), formerly thought of as cave-dwellers because the Hebrew word hōr means "cave," are now known to have been the non-Semitic Hurrians, a people who lived at Nuzi and elsewhere. The Amalekites (14:7) lived in the Negev and in the Sinai peninsula, while the Amorites (14:7) lived in Canaan and northern Mesopotamia.

The Dead Sea region became the scene of a battle in which four powerful northern kings emerged victorious over five rebellious southern kings who had been their vassals. When the northern kings took plunder from Sodom and Gomorrah they also seized captives, among whom was Abram's nephew, Lot (14:12).

By now Lot was "living in Sodom," and this was his *third* downward step. He had moved right into town and was living among the wicked people of Sodom. Interestingly enough, although Lot lived in Sodom, its citizens apparently never considered him to be really one of them, because in 19:9 they call him an "alien." Maybe 2 Peter 2:7, 8 provides a clue to Lot's status; the passage states three times that Lot was "righteous," in contrast to the men of Sodom who were "sensual," "unprincipled" and "lawless."

A fugitive from the defeated side in the battle came and told Abram that Lot had been captured. So, together with his allies and 318 trained men, Abram pursued the enemy as far as Dan (14:14). Genesis 14:14 is a fascinating verse for the historian, because it contains a unique and very old Hebrew word ("trained men," perhaps better translated "armed retainers")[7] as well as a late editorial touch Dan, the well-known city in the north of Palestine, was not so named until the time of Israel's judges (see Judg. 18:29).

Abram's wealth and power are well illustrated in this story. He had 318 men capable of bearing arms at his beck and call. And that was a formidable enough force to rout the enemy and retrieve the plunder and captives including, of course, the unfortunate Lot.

Genesis 14:18-20 is a brief but very important interlude in the story. It gives us a few tantalizing details about a man named Melchizedek. He was a Canaanite priest of *El Elyon* ("God Most High"); El was the chief deity in the Canaanite pantheon. Melchizedek was also the king of Salem (a shortened form of "Jerusalem"; see Ps. 76:2). In ancient times, priestly and kingly duties were often executed by a single individual. Melchizedek blessed Abram, who responded by giving him a tenth (tithe) of the plunder. (The patriarchs recognized the importance of the tithe; we'll observe this fact again in Gen. 28:22, where Jacob promised to pay to God a tithe of all he possessed.)

As a Canaanite priest, Melchizedek was evidently a pagan.

But Abram, recognizing in him the potential of becoming a believer in the one true God, identified Melchizedek's "God Most High" with "the LORD" (14:22). Since it is the Lord alone who deserves the title "God Most High," Abram in effect was acknowledging that Melchizedek was genuinely seeking God's will. And since giving a tithe is a spiritual act, Abram probably would not have given one to Melchizedek if he had not considered Melchizedek a man spiritually worthy of receiving it.

Melchizedek figures prominently in the New Testament in Hebrews 4:14–7:28 (and especially 7:1-28). In that passage, Genesis 14:18-20 is alluded to several times and Psalm 110:4 (the only other biblical passage referring to Melchizedek) is directly quoted several times. The point of the argument in Hebrews is that Melchizedek is a prefiguration or type of Christ, our great High Priest. The priesthood of Jesus is, therefore, "according to the order of Melchizedek" rather than "according to the order of Aaron." Since Melchizedek lived centuries earlier than Aaron, his priesthood must be greater than that of Aaron. And since the Jewish priests of Jesus' time were priests in Aaron's order, Jesus was greater than any of them because only He was a priest in Melchizedek's order.

(Another proof that Melchizedek was greater than Aaron, according to Hebrews 7, is that Abram, Aaron's ancestor, paid a tithe to Melchizedek. Aaron, therefore, also in effect paid a tithe to Melchizedek, since Aaron's ancestor Levi was in the loins of Abram at the time! If all of this sounds a bit complicated, study Hebrews 7 carefully. The author's arguments are easy to follow, and other comparisons between Melchizedek and Jesus as well as contrasts between the priesthoods of Melchizedek and Aaron are clearly set forth.)

But for now we must get back to the final verses of Genesis 14. After his meeting with Melchizedek, Abram returned to the king of Sodom to restore the plunder and captives to him. The king said to him, "Give the people to me and take the goods for yourself." He apparently felt that Abram deserved a sizable payment for having routed the northern kings and retrieved the plunder.

But Abram responded that he had taken an oath to the Lord not to keep anything belonging to the king or people of Sodom.

The Hebrew text of Genesis 14:22 reminds us that the means of oath-taking in ancient times was lifting one's hand (see also Deut. 32:40; Rev. 10:5,6), a practice still followed in modern courtroom procedure. To paraphrase Abram a bit, he said: "I have raised my right hand on solemn oath to the Lord that I would keep absolutely nothing belonging to you. I do have some allies, so give them their expenses, but don't pay me anything. I don't want you to be able to claim that you made me rich."

We should not understand this to mean that the laborer is unworthy of his hire. It is important for us to observe that Abram was *already* a wealthy man, as we've noted before. Also, we might compare Abram's situation with that of Elisha in 2 Kings 5. Just as Elisha refused to accept gifts from the commander-in-chief of Syria's army (2 Kings 5:16), so did Abram refuse to accept favors from Sodom's king. Both men trusted ultimately in God alone—and so should we.

These three chapters of Genesis describe Abram's travels through quite a bit of the land of Canaan. But although the promise of inheriting the land was given to him and to his descendants, he himself received not one square foot of it (Acts 7:5). He simply had to accept God's statements on faith. He had to trust that the God who had promised was also a God who would keep His word.

Footnotes

1. C. Percy in *Parade* magazine, February 17, 1974, p. 11.
2. *Newsweek* magazine, September 17, 1973, p. 51.
3. *Time* magazine, August 12, 1974, p. 78.
4. See N. M. Sarna, *Understanding Genesis* (New York: Schocken Books, 1970), p. 226.
5. K. Kitchen in C. F. H. Henry, ed., *Dictionary of Christian Ethics* (Washington, D. C.: Canon Press, 1973), p. 202.
6. K. Kitchen, *Ancient Orient and Old Testament* (Chicago: Inter-Varsity Press, 1966), pp. 79, 80.
7. See W. F. Albright, *Yahweh and the Gods of Canaan* (Garden City: Doubleday & Company, Inc., 1968), pp. 69, 70.

3

ABRAM:

His Covenant
Genesis 15:1—17:27

Genesis 14 ends with Abram's forfeit of all claim to the plunder that he had retrieved from the four northern kings (Gen. 14:22-24). He didn't want the king of Sodom to be able to boast about having made him rich.

Genesis 15 begins with the Lord's reassurance to Abram that he was rich beyond measure. This was not because of the gold and silver and animals and servants that Abram possessed, but because God Himself was Abram's treasure (15:1). When the Lord promises to be our treasure, financial reverses or other similar problems are easier to bear. The Levites would learn this fact centuries later (Deut. 10:9), and God wanted Abram to learn it right now.

The Covenant Established—15:1-21
For the fourth time in four chapters of Genesis (see Gen. 12:1-3; 12:7; 13:14-17; and now 15:1), God spoke to Abram. We

cannot be absolutely certain that it was in an audible voice, but we suspect that it was; we know that audible conversations between God and His choicest servants did take place (see 1 Sam. 3:4-14). The patriarchs enjoyed an intimate relationship with their God. The atmosphere was often conversational; they chatted together about matters that were mutually important to them.

But Abram was not satisfied with God's comments in Genesis 15:1. Abram had other concerns: he was getting old, he had no sons of his own, and Eliezer of Damascus, one of his household slaves whose services he may have acquired on the way southward from Haran (see 12:5), would inherit Abram's entire estate!

Why so? Well, the Nuzi documents illustrate the fact that if a man did not have a son of his own, he could legally adopt a young man and pass his inheritance on to his newly adopted son. Very often the adopted son would be one of the man's servants, a servant he had come to know and trust, a servant who had perhaps already demonstrated his dependability around the household in a variety of ways.

Apparently that's what had happened here; because his wife Sarai was sterile (11:30), Abram had adopted Eliezer as his son and was now unhappy that he would be his heir. But God spoke again and assured Abram that Eliezer would *not* be his heir. On the contrary, a son issuing from Abram's own body would be his heir (15:4).

Once again, the Nuzi documents supply a helpful explanation of patriarchal custom. They illustrate the fact that if the man of the house eventually had a son of his own, the rights of that son would supersede the rights of the adopted son. In other words, Eliezer's rights to Abram's property were not absolute or inviolable; if Abram should have a son of his own, Eliezer's claim would be invalidated.

So God promised Abram that he would have his own son. That promise would be fulfilled in Abram's old age when Isaac was born (21:2). Isaac would be the son "of promise" (Gal. 4:28), and we who belong to Jesus Christ are children of promise, Isaac's spiritual descendants, as Paul declares in Galatians 4:21-31.

God further promised Abram that his offspring would be as numerous as the stars in the sky (Gen. 15:5). In the pitch blackness of the Near Eastern night, unillumined by any artificial light, Abram could look up and see thousands of stars. He would become weary indeed if he tried to count them all. And that's how many descendants he, already an old man with no children, was going to have!

That promise was repeated to Abram in 22:17 after he had demonstrated his obedience to God by being willing to offer up Isaac as a sacrifice. And that promise was fulfilled at the time of the people of Israel's entrance into Canaan (Deut. 1:10). The New Testament writers marveled at the promise, which is mentioned in Romans 4:18 and which Hebrews 11:12 confirms as having been fulfilled.

But we must constantly remind ourselves that Abram's descendants are often a spiritual rather than a physical entity in New Testament references. Galatians 3:29 states that people who belong to Christ are Abram's offspring. And Revelation 7:9, using language reminiscent of Genesis 15:5, refers to a huge ingathering of God's people at the end of time, "a great multitude, which no one could count, from every nation and all tribes and peoples and tongues."

Abram's response to God's promise was one of faith. We are told that he "believed in the LORD" (Gen. 15:6). This is the first use of the verb "believe" in the Bible, and Genesis 15:6 gives us a beautiful and concise definition of what faith is all about. "Faith" means "belief in God," "believing what God tells us." And Abram was "the father of all who believe" (Rom. 4:11), the spiritual father of everyone who has ever had saving faith.

In a real sense, the wording of Genesis 15:6 describes Abram's conversion. The verse is so important that the New Testament writers quoted it several times. It appears in whole or in part three times in Romans 4 (4:3, 22, 23) as well as in Galatians 3:6 and James 2:23.

In Romans 4:23-25, Abram's faith is compared with our faith in the death and resurrection of Christ. In other words, his faith in what God had told him up to that point is placed on the same level as our faith in what God has told us and revealed to us through Christ. In Galatians 3:6, 7, we learn that it is believers in general who are children of Abraham. And in James 2:23, Genesis 15:6 is quoted as proof that faith apart from works is dead. If we don't prove our faith by working for Christ and living as He wants us to live, our faith isn't worth much; it's as good as dead.

James 2:23 also calls Abram "the friend of God," a name also applied to him in 2 Chronicles 20:7 and Isaiah 41:8. Believers in God are God's special friends! Abram lived in or near Hebron for much of his life, and the modern Arabic name for Hebron is *El-Khalîl*, "the friend"—a beautiful reference to Abram.

When Abram believed in the Lord, the Lord credited that faith to him as righteousness (Gen. 15:6). Like Abram, we have no genuine righteousness of our own. All our righteousness has to be credited or imputed to us, and that can happen only as a result of our faith (Heb. 10:38; 11:7), our believing in God and His word.

Now, a covenant scene develops before our eyes. Exodus 20:1-17, the Ten Commandments, exhibits a literary outline similar to that of Hittite treaties coming from the period of c. 1450 to c. 1200 B. C.[1] The elements are (1) the self-identification of the king, in this case "I am the LORD your God" (20:2); (2) the historical prologue, in this case "who brought you out of the land of Egypt, out of the house of slavery" (20:2); and (3) the stipulations of the covenant, in this case the Ten Commandments themselves (20:3-17).

Genesis 15:7 exhibits the first two elements in a strikingly similar way: (1) "I am the LORD," and (2) "who brought you out of Ur of the Chaldeans, to give you this land to possess it." These elements tend to mark out the scene before us as a covenant scene, a fact that would be confirmed later in Genesis 15.

Abram's response to God's promise this time was one of doubt rather than faith (15:8). How characteristic this is! Even people of great faith experience their moments of doubt. Living the life of faith is not like starting at the bottom of an escalator that always and continually moves upward to heaven. It's more like riding a roller-coaster with its hills and valleys. In Genesis 15:6 Abram was on the mountaintop; in 15:8 he was down in the valley, doubting. "How may I know that I shall possess it?"

Zacharias, soon to be the father of John the Baptist, would ask a very similar question centuries after Abram's time (Luke 1:18). In fact, it was a characteristic of Abram's descendants to "ask for signs" (1 Cor. 1:22)!

So God, in His great condescension, told Abram to go and get certain animals three years of age, and two birds as well. Three years was the prime age for most animals used in sacrifices (see 1 Sam. 1:24). Abram was then told to cut the animals in half and line them up in two rows (Gen. 15:10). He didn't cut the birds in half, however, apparently because they were too small (see also Lev. 1:17). (At Mari on the Euphrates, the donkey was used as the main sacrificial animal to solemnize covenants during the patriarchal period.[2] The animals used by Abram at God's command were a heifer, a female goat, and a ram.)

At sunset, Abram fell into a deep sleep, during which the LORD told him his descendants would live for 400 years in a foreign land where they would be enslaved and exploited. That land (Egypt, as later events demonstrated) would in turn be judged, however, and then Abram's descendants would return to Canaan (see also Gen. 46:4). Stephen's historical summary in Acts mentioned these important events (Acts 7:6,7,17).

Abram was told that his descendants would come back "in the fourth generation" (Gen. 15:16). Apparently a "generation," usually referring to the age of a man when his first son is born, was considered to be a hundred years in length during the patriarchal period. This tallies well with the statement that Abraham was a hundred years old when Isaac, his firstborn son from the legal standpoint, was born (21:5). In turn, the 400 years of 15:13 is perhaps a round number for the 430 years of Exodus 12:40, "the time that the sons of Israel lived in Egypt."

Abram's descendants would be able to return to Canaan only when the iniquity of the Amorite inhabitants of the land was "complete" (Gen. 15:16). God would not destroy the Amorites until they were ripe for judgment and destruction. From their own epic literature—discovered at the site of ancient Ugarit on the Syrian coast beginning in 1929—we have learned a great deal about just how wicked many of the so-called religious practices of the Canaanites were.[3] God is merciful, but His longsuffering and forbearance are not granted to people indefinitely. When

32

stubborn disobedience passes the point of no return, God punishes the sinner.

In the meantime, God promised Abram that he would not die until he had reached a good old age (15:15), a promise that He kept, as always (25:7, 8). The Canaanites would be punished, but Abram would be rewarded. And it is just as true now as it was then: God judges sin, but He honors righteousness.

Genesis 15 concludes with an eerie but highly significant scene. Darkness came across the land while Abram was still apparently sound asleep. Suddenly, "a smoking oven and a flaming torch" (15:17) passed between the halves of the animals that Abram had earlier slaughtered and arranged in two rows (15:10). The oven and torch marched, as it were, down the aisle formed by the animal parts. This was a solemn ceremony confirming and solemnizing the covenant about to be established (see especially Jer. 34:18, 19). In such ancient ceremonies, a participant in a covenant would vow something like this: "If I violate the terms of this covenant, may what happened to these animals happen to me!" Obviously, covenants were not entered into lightly or unadvisedly in ancient times.

The oven and torch undoubtedly symbolized the presence of God, as fire often does in the Bible (see Exod. 3:2; 14:24; 19:18; 1 Kings 18:38; Acts 2:3,4). There were two main types of covenant in ancient times: suzerainty and parity. Covenants between equals were parity covenants, while those between a superior and an inferior were suzerainty covenants.[4] Needless to say, all covenants between God and man in the Bible are suzerainty rather than parity covenants. In Abram's case, God, the Suzerain, established the covenant and was the active participant; Abram, the vassal, received the covenant and was the passive participant. His passive role is stressed by the fact that he remained asleep during the entire transaction!

Once again we observe the condescension of our God. As He symbolically passed between the pieces of the slaughtered animals, He in effect was laying His own reputation on the line. He was expressing His willingness to accept the fate of those animals if He should break His covenant promise.

The Lord, as the Suzerain, "made" (15:18) the covenant with Abram. The verb "made" means literally "cut" and refers to the

33

sacrifice that accompanied formal covenants in the Old Testament period (see Ps. 50:5). To "cut" a covenant meant to establish or make a covenant.

The covenant terms that God made with Abram included the promise that He would give his descendants the territory that began at the eastern border of Egypt and stretched all the way to the Euphrates river. Abram's descendants did, in fact, receive that land during the Old Testament period. The Israelites were commanded to go in and take it (Deut. 1:7, 8), they did so under the leadership of Joshua (Josh. 21:43), and they lived in it during the days of Solomon (1 Kings 4:20, 21). So God's promise of land was fulfilled already in ancient times.

That doesn't mean that it can't be fulfilled more than once, of course. For example, whether the modern state of Israel is a further fulfillment of the patriarchal promise is a question that is being hotly debated in our day. Modern Israel may well be such a fulfillment, but it need not be the *only* fulfillment.

The ceremony solemnizing the covenant with Abram was intended to confirm to Abram that what God had promised He would surely fulfill. It was the sign Abram had asked for (Gen. 15:8). And one further point: covenants in the Bible were always solemnized by blood. There is no such thing as a biblical covenant without a blood sacrifice. This fact has supremely important implications for us as well, since our covenant relationship to Christ was sealed with His own precious blood. We are reminded of His words of institution at the last supper: "This cup is the new covenant in My blood" (1 Cor. 11:25).

The Covenant Ignored—16:1-16

Land and people—that was the twofold promise implied in God's covenant with Abram. They cannot be separated, because without the land the people are homeless and without the people the land is unfulfilled. So Holy Land and Holy People go together.

Now Abram and Sarai knew that God had promised Abram a son (Gen. 15:4). But Sarai, as before (11:30), was still barren (16:1). So she made a proposal to Abram that, by our standards, was shocking: "Go in to my maid; perhaps I shall obtain children through her" (16:2). It was a proposal that the wives of

34

her grandson, Jacob, would later repeat to him (30:3,4,9).

How in the world could the wives of the patriarchs suggest such a thing? Once again, as the documents from Nuzi illustrate, it was the legally authorized custom of that time for a man who had no son to take measures that would insure the orderly disposition of his inheritance when he died. He could adopt a son, as Abram had apparently already done (see 15:2,3). Or, according to Nuzi law, he could produce a son by cohabiting with one of the servant girls in his household. And if a son were in fact born as a result of such cohabitation, the inheritance rights of that son would supersede the rights of any previously adopted son. In a polygamous society, where men commonly had a wife and one or more concubines (as Abram did; see 25:6), cohabiting with a servant girl was not so strange or shocking as it might seem to us.

But just because it was commonly done does not mean that God condoned it. Abram and Sarai were trying to help God out, in a sense; they were demonstrating their own impatience. They felt that Sarai's old age formed a barrier to God's power.

So when Sarai spoke, Abram hearkened (16:2)—just as Adam had to Eve (3:17). And the result was tragic in both cases. Rivalry arose between the two wives, Sarai and Hagar, the Egyptian servant girl (16:4). Sarai became angry with Abram because of Hagar's impertinence (16:5). Finally, Sarai mistreated Hagar so severely that she was forced to run away while still pregnant (16:6). All of these unfortunate circumstances took place because Abram and Sarai were impatient and disobedient.

Hagar naturally headed westward toward Egypt. She stopped at a spring of water on the way to Shur, a site located east of Egypt (25:18; 1 Sam. 15:7). There the angel of the Lord found her and talked to her (Gen. 16:7-12).

Who was the angel of the Lord? Many answers have been given to this question.[5] In Genesis 16:13 he seems to be equated with the Lord Himself, and so some people have taught that the angel of the Lord was really Jesus Christ in a pre-incarnation form.

Since the Hebrew word for "angel" also means "messenger," other commentators explain that the angel of the Lord was a special messenger from the court of heaven who bore the credentials of the King of heaven and could therefore speak on His behalf. This was the case with other messengers in ancient times; they had the right and the authority to speak on behalf of the one who had sent them forth. They symbolized the presence of the king who had given them their mission.

Judges 13 is a very instructive passage in this regard. There the angel is called "the angel of the LORD" (13:3, 13, 15-18, 20, 21), a "man of God" (13:6, 8), "the angel of God" (13:6, 9), a "man" (13:10,11), "God" (13:22) and "the LORD" (13:23). He could hardly bear all of these titles at once unless he looked like a man but at the same time was a messenger representing someone else. When the "angel" or "messenger" of the Lord appeared, then, the Lord Himself was present.

Since Hagar believed that seeing the angel of the Lord was tantamount to seeing the Lord Himself, she reacted with surprise (Gen. 16:13). Like Jacob many years later (32:30), she wondered how it was possible for her to actually see God without being severely judged for it. In memory of the event, the well where the meeting took place was named *Beer-lahai-roi*. If it was named from God's standpoint, it means "the well of the one who sees Me and lives"; if named from Hagar's standpoint, it means "the well of the Living One who sees me." Either translation is possible, but the first would seem to be the most likely in context.

But why did the angel intercept Hagar in the first place? He wanted to tell her to go back to Sarai, to tell her that she would have many descendants, that God had "heard" her cry of affliction (16:11), and that she would bear a son named *Ishmael* which means "God hears." (Gen. 17:20 contains a similar pun on Ishmael's name.) We may sometimes feel that God is unconcerned about us, but He is faithful and always hears and "sees" (Exod. 3:7) the affliction of His people.

And so it was that Abram, at 86 years of age (Gen. 16:16), became the father of Ishmael. As there was antagonism between Hagar and Sarai (16:4-6), so there would be (16:12) between Ishmael (and his descendants) and Sarai's own firstborn son, Isaac (and his descendants). But that still lay in the future. For now, we can be sure that Abram rejoiced in the birth of Ishmael, believing that he was the fulfillment of God's promise as stated in 15:4.

The Covenant Sealed—17:1-27

Thirteen years later (17:1) the Lord again appeared to Abram in a covenant context, just as He had to Abram in 15:7 and just as He would to Moses and the people of Israel centuries later (Exod. 20:2). He revealed Himself to Abram by a new name, *El Shaddai* (Gen. 17:1), which is usually translated as "God Almighty." It was the special name that God used to reveal Himself to the patriarchs, as Exodus 6:3 points out. The name is found many times throughout the rest of Genesis, and *Shaddai* alone occurs most commonly in the book of Job (who was himself a patriarchal figure). *El Shaddai* may mean literally "God, the Mountain One," as many recent scholars assert.[6] But it came to have the meaning of "God Almighty" because it describes the God who makes things happen by means of His majestic power and might.

God came to Abram and wanted him, like Noah before him (Gen. 6:9) and believers in Thessalonica after him (1 Thess. 5:23), to walk before Him and be blameless (Gen. 17:1). The Lord can best use people who are willing to live godly lives in His sight.

Now God confirmed His covenant with Abram (17:2). Unlike the earlier covenant with Noah (9:8-17), this covenant was conditional on the obedience of Abram and his descendants (17:1,9; 18:19; 22:18; 26:4,5; Deut. 30:15-20). From God's standpoint all covenants are eternal (Gen. 17:7,13), but from man's standpoint they can be broken (Isa. 24:5; Jer. 31:32). When we break God's covenants, we also break His heart, because then He has to punish us, which is something He doesn't take delight in doing (2 Pet. 3:9). The covenant at Mt. Sinai was also conditional (Exod. 19:5), but unfortunately the people of Israel broke it innumerable times throughout their long history, and God therefore had to judge them for their sin over and over again.

We observe once more the twin poles of the covenant promises to Abram: land (Gen. 17:8), and descendants (17:2, 4-6, 16, 20). As the land received the major emphasis in Genesis 15, so the descendants receive it in Genesis 17.

God changed Abram's name to Abraham (17:5), a fact noted by Nehemiah in his summary of Israel's history (Neh. 9:7).

Abram means "Exalted Father," a reference not to Abram himself but to God. Many names in ancient times contained the name of a deity, and "Father" was a commonly used divine element in such names. For example, "*Ab*ijah" means "my *Father* is the LORD," and "Eli*ab*" means "my God is *Father.*" The *ab*-element in such Hebrew names meant "Father" in reference to God, so that "Exalted *Father,*" the meaning of "*Ab*ram," refers to God Himself rather than to Abram, the man who bore the name.

When Abram's name was changed to "Abraham," a rather beautiful twist took place. The *ab*-element now referred to Abram himself, who received the new name "*Ab*raham," which means "*father* of a multitude" (Gen. 17:5). The new name reflected his new status as promised him by God—he would become "the father of a multitude of nations."

Having Abraham as one's ancestor could become an unfortunate source of pride in later generations (see Matt. 3:9). But the ultimate intention of God's covenant promise to Abraham was sensed by Paul, who emphasized the *spiritual* aspect of Abraham's fatherhood to both Jew and Gentile (Rom. 4:17; Gal. 3:29).

From the *physical* standpoint the covenant also had meaning, of course. Kings would descend from Abraham (Gen. 17:6), a prediction to be fulfilled during the days of the Israelite monarchies (see also Deut. 17:14-20, a description of what those kings would be like if they were diligent in following God's will).

But most important of all was the fact that the Lord promised to be the God of Abraham and his descendants (Gen. 17:7,8). The statement, "I will be their God, and they shall be My people," became a prominent and characteristic phrase in covenant contexts (Jer. 31:33; 24:7; Ezek. 34:30; Hos. 2:23; Zech. 8:8). This is only as it should be, because a covenant is an agreement that stands or falls on the basis of *personal relationship.* If the signatories are not trustworthy, if they fail to love and respect each other, the covenant isn't worth the material it's written on.

As the rainbow is the sign of the Noahic covenant (Gen. 9:13), and as the sabbath is the sign of the Sinaitic covenant (Exod. 31:16,17) so circumcision became the sign of the Abrahamic covenant (Gen. 17:11). The rainbow and the sabbath were already in existence prior to the institution of the covenants they came to signify. So also circumcision did not originate with Abraham. It was practiced in Egypt and elsewhere centuries before his time,[7] but it was invested with new meaning in Genesis 17. In much the same way, thousands of people were crucified before the time of Jesus, but the cross took on a vastly new and different meaning when our Lord was crucified.

Circumcision symbolizes the removal of uncleanness, and so the word is sometimes used in the figurative sense of the removal of ethical or spiritual uncleanness, as in Deuteronomy 10:16 (of the heart) or in Jeremiah 6:10 (where uncircumcised ears are mentioned). The circumcision of Genesis 17, then, though literal and physical, would become more meaningful to Israel through her long history because of its added ethical and spiritual significance.

In the epistles of Paul, physical circumcision loses its importance entirely. Spiritual circumcision, which involves faith in Christ coupled with moral purity, becomes predominant (see Rom. 2:28, 29; 1 Cor. 7:19; Gal. 5:6; Col. 3:11; and especially Phil. 3:3).

But physical circumcision became the badge of Abraham's male descendants, and the practice in his case began with Abraham himself and all the male members of his household. Abraham at the age of 99 and Ishmael at the age of 13 were circumcised along with all the others—and we observe again the promptness with which Abraham obeyed God's command (Gen. 17:23, 26). From that time on, every male child in Abraham's line was circumcised (17:12) as Jewish baby boys still are today.

The operation is performed on the organ of reproduction because the covenant emphasized the procreation of descendants. The implication is clear: if the foreskin was not cut off, then the individual himself would be cut off from the people of God because the covenant would have been broken (17:14). The image was a very vivid one. And, perhaps not so incidentally, the operation itself reminds us again that covenants are solemnized only through the shedding of blood.

In addition to Abraham, two others played a role in the

covenant drama, Sarai, his wife, had her name changed also—to "Sarah," a name that, like *Sarai,* means "Princess." Clearly, in her case the change of name was not so significant as was that of Abraham, although it did reflect the fact that she would become "a mother of nations" (17:16).

For the first time, Abraham was now told that Sarah would bear a son and so share in the blessing of Abraham's descendants. Incredible! A 100-year-old man and a 90-year-old woman to have a child of their own? It was too much for Abraham and so he "laughed" (17:17). But the boy would be born in spite of Abraham's doubt, and "Isaac," which means "he laughs," would be his name (17:19). (We'll read about further puns on Isaac's name in 18:12-15 and 21:6.)

The other actor in the drama was Ishmael. Because of Abraham's lack of faith, he wanted Ishmael to enjoy God's favor. But God had other plans, as we have already seen. Nevertheless, Ishmael would be blessed as well (17:20) and would become the ancestor of twelve chieftains (a prediction fulfilled in 25:12-16). He was not the son of promise, however. That honor went to Isaac.

As we've read Genesis 15—17, we've observed that Abraham wavered between faith and unbelief. If he, the spiritual father of believers, could do so and still be called a "friend of God," there is yet hope for us.

Footnotes

1. See conveniently G. E. Mendenhall in E. F. Campbell, Jr. and D. N. Freedman, *The Biblical Archaeologist Reader, 3* (Garden City: Doubleday Anchor, 1970), pp. 32-42.

2. See W. F. Albright in J. B. Pritchard, ed., *Ancient Near Eastern Texts,* second edition (Princeton: Princeton University Press, 1955), p. 482, note 4.

3. See, for example, the analysis of W. F. Albright in *Archaeology and the Religion of Israel,* fourth edition (Baltimore: Johns Hopkins, 1956), pp. 71-84.

4. G. E. Mendenhall in *op. cit.,* pp. 28-32.

5. For a convenient summary see G. F. Oehler, *Theology of the Old Testament* (Grand Rapids: Zondervan reprint, undated), pp. 129-134.

6. See W. F. Albright, *Yahweh and the Gods of Canaan* (Garden City: Doubleday & Company, Inc., 1968), pp. 188, 189.

7. See, for example, H. O. Forshey in *Restoration Quarterly* 16/3-4 (1973), pp. 151-153.

ABRAHAM:

His Family
Genesis 18:1—21:34

Genesis 15—17, the section on the Abrahamic covenant, forms a bridge between Genesis 12—14 (which is concerned mainly with the promise of land) and Genesis 18—21 (which is concerned mainly with Abraham's family). The Abrahamic covenant itself focuses on the twin concerns of land and family. Our purpose in studying Genesis 18—21 will be to observe what happened in subsequent history to several members of Abraham's family and clan.

The Destruction of Sodom and Gomorrah—18:1—19:38

One hot afternoon, the Lord again "appeared" to Abraham in the person of "three men" (Gen. 18:1,2).

The keynote of Genesis 18:1-8 and 19:1-3 is hospitality. Hebrews 13:2 is probably a reflection of these incidents: "Do not neglect to show hospitality to strangers, for by this some have entertained angels without knowing it." Genuine hospitality is almost a lost art in many circles today. But in the ancient Near East it was a quality that characterized every host and was expected by every guest. That same quality can also be observed in many areas of modern Palestine.

In Abraham's case, he bowed down to greet his visitors, welcomed them courteously, brought water to wash the dust from their feet, and presented them with a sumptuous meal. And he took care of all their needs quickly: he "ran" (Gen. 18:2), he "hurried" (18:6), he "ran" (18:7). He did everything he could to make them feel right at home, to give them the personal attention they deserved. There are lessons in abundance for us here, because to the extent that our lives become more impersonal, to that extent we become less hospitable.

From inside the tent where she couldn't be seen, Sarah overheard the word of the Lord to Abraham as mediated through the three men: "Sarah your wife shall have a son" (18:10). This was the first inkling Sarah had of God's incredible promise. Before, when Abraham heard it for the first time, he had laughed (17:16, 17). Now, it was Sarah's turn to laugh. After all, at 90 she was already much too old to have children.

But the Lord was displeased, not only with Sarah's laughter but also with her subsequent denial that she had laughed. He asked Abraham, "Is anything too difficult [wonderful, miraculous] for the LORD?" (18:14). We sometimes forget just how powerful our God is! An angel had to remind the virgin Mary of the same truth concerning her own pregnancy and that of her aged kinswoman, Elizabeth: "Nothing will be impossible with God" (Luke 1:37). Can Mary, a virgin, conceive? Of course! Can an elderly woman become pregnant? Absolutely!

But how about in the spiritual realm? Can sinners be saved? Yes, we can, praise God, because here, too, "with God all things are possible" (Matt. 19:25, 26)! Salvation is the greatest miracle of all, a miracle that every true believer in Christ has experienced. And it makes Sarah's forthcoming pregnancy pale by comparison!

When Abraham's guests got ready to leave for Sodom, he walked along with them for a short distance (Gen. 18:16). The Lord decided to tell Abraham of His plans to destroy Sodom and Gomorrah because He didn't want to hide those plans from him. After all, Abraham was God's friend (2 Chron. 20:7; Isa. 41:8; Jas. 2:23), and good friends often share intimate secrets with each

42

other. Abraham was also a "prophet" (Gen. 20:7), and God does nothing without disclosing His plans to His servants the prophets (Amos 3:7).

The wickedness of Sodom and Gomorrah was already well known (Gen. 13:13). It would become proverbial in later generations (see, for example, Ezek. 16:49, 50). The Lord was therefore going down to look the situation over (Gen. 18:21), just as He had done in the days of the building of the Tower of Babel (11:5). He had entrusted that mission to His faithful messengers, Abraham's guests (18:16, 22; 19:1).

By now, Abraham had come to realize that the destruction of Sodom was a live possibility. So he was determined to intercede for its people, particularly Lot. The result is one of the most famous and boldest intercessory prayers in all of Scripture (18:23-32). His eloquent plea demonstrated the fact that the prayer of a righteous man does, in fact, reach the waiting ear of God and make its impact on people and events (Jas. 5:16).

In his prayer, Abraham was not bargaining with God, as it is often thought. He knew God to be a just and honest Judge (Gen. 18:25), as Moses would also learn to know Him (Deut. 32:4). And he knew himself, by comparison, to be nothing but dust and ashes (Gen. 18:27). Abraham knew very well how important it is to be humble in the presence of a sovereign God (see Isa. 2:11,17; 5:15,16; Mic. 6:8).

But Abraham nevertheless persevered in his plea, asking God to spare Sodom for the sake of 50 righteous people in it (if that many could be found there), then 45, then 40, then 30, then 20, and finally 10. And God promised that if only 10 righteous people could be found in Sodom, He would indeed spare the city.

It may be that Abraham stopped at the number ten because he had been doing some mental arithmetic while praying. Perhaps he had counted Lot, his wife, at least two sons (Gen. 19:12), at least two married daughters and their husbands (19:14), and two unmarried daughters (19:8)—exactly ten! And even if the daughters of 19:14 had not yet married their fiances and were the same as the daughters of 19:8—couldn't two other righteous people be found somewhere else in Sodom? Of course! The city was safe!

But when two of the three angel-messengers who had visited Abraham arrived in Sodom, it soon became apparent that Lot himself had become deeply involved in the life of the city. He was sitting in the gateway of Sodom, which probably meant that he was a member of the ruling council there (see Ruth 4:1,2,11 for an example of the prosecution of legal matters in a city gateway, often used as a courtroom in ancient times). If Lot was indeed one of Sodom's ruling elders, that fact would constitute his *fourth* step downward, spiritually speaking. (For the first three, see again Gen. 13:11; 13:12; and 14:12.)

As Abraham had done earlier, Lot extended hospitality toward his guests. He invited them into his house for a hearty meal and a good night's sleep (19:2,3). And now the wickedness of Sodom's male citizens was revealed in all its horror: they demanded that Lot bring his two guests outside to them so they could commit homosexual acts against them (see Jude 7). This immoral practice was so characteristic of Sodom's men that homosexuality is often called "sodomy" even today. The Bible always and everywhere states that homosexuality is sin, and no amount of propaganda to the contrary by so-called "gay liberation" movements here and abroad can change that basic fact.

Lot refused to release his guests to the lust of his neighbors, but he did agree to allow the Sodomites to abuse his two virgin daughters if they so desired (Gen. 19:8). This incredible offer constituted Lot's *fifth* step downward. But the Sodomites did not even want the daughters—they wanted only Lot's male guests! The whole sordid incident has its counterpart later on in the period of the judges (see Judg. 19:22-26), during a time when "everyone did what was right in his own eyes" (Judg. 21:25). "Do to [my daughters] whatever you like," Lot had said (Gen. 19:8). And so it goes—when God's sovereignty is denied and His laws are ignored, anarchy reigns and sinful people take over.

Poor, unfortunate Lot! Apparently the men of Sodom never did consider him to be one of them (despite his own spiritual problems, he did not sink to the Sodomites' lowest level; see 2 Pet. 2:7,8). He was recognized as a foreigner and accused of setting himself up as a judge (Gen. 19:9), as Moses was centuries later (Exod. 2:14). When the Sodomites became determined to

44

break down the door of Lot's house in order to get at his guests, the guests struck them blind so they couldn't even find the door.

Sodom's wickedness made it ripe for judgment and annihilation. The Lord's messengers told Lot to take all his relatives out of the city to escape the coming destruction. When Lot relayed the message to his sons-in-law they thought he was joking, so low had his witness and credibility slipped by that time—and that loss of the power of moral persuasion constituted Lot's *sixth* downward step.

By now, apparently, only four righteous people were left in Sodom instead of the ten required to save it: Lot, his wife, and their two unmarried daughters. The destruction of the city was now inevitable, so the angels urged the four to run for their lives. When Lot hesitated (would he have to leave some of his prized possessions in Sodom?), the men took the four by the hand and led them out of town. In so doing, they demonstrated God's mercy to them (Gen. 19:16). People who are blind, whether spiritually or physically, need the gentle hand of the Lord to lead them out of their difficulties (see especially Mark 8:23).

But Lot still balked. He didn't want to go into the hills outside of town, because he didn't think he could get there in time. So he requested shelter from the destruction in a nearby village. Because Lot stressed the smallness of the village (and therefore the smallness of his request!) more than once (Gen. 19:20), its name became *Zoar,* which means "small." The Lord agreed to Lot's request, and once again we catch a glimpse of His grace and love. He allows Himself to be limited by His people's foibles: "I cannot do anything until you arrive there" (19:22).

As soon as Lot reached Zoar, the Lord destroyed Sodom, Gomorrah and all the other towns of the plain (Zoar alone excepted) in a fiery holocaust. The catastrophe was remembered by later generations as a clear example of divine judgment (Isa. 13:19; Lam. 4:6; Jude 7). It was often compared in severity and scope to the judgment on mankind by the great flood in the days of Noah (Luke 17:26-30; 2 Pet. 2:5-8).

When Lot's wife looked back to watch the awful scene (was she, too, concerned about leaving her prized possessions behind?), she became a pillar of salt, perhaps soon indistinguishable from the innumerable grotesque salt formations found near

45

the southern end of the Dead Sea to this day. Her fate also became proverbial in its own right. The memory of Lot's wife serves as a reminder to us not to turn back, no matter how temptingly the things of this world may beckon (Luke 17:32). Her hesitation cost her everything she had, including her very life.

So Sodom was destroyed—but, in spite of that, Abraham's prayer was answered! Lot had been spared, and that was the basic motive behind Abraham's prayer in the first place (Gen. 19:29). Our prayers are not always answered in the way we might expect or prefer. Nevertheless, they are in fact always answered, but always in God's way, which is always the best way.

Genesis 19:30-38 is a section that details the *seventh* and last downward step that Lot took: an incestuous relationship with his two daughters. To be sure, his role was passive; they gave him wine to drink, and then they cohabited with him while he was in a drunken stupor. But he had obviously not brought them up in the nurture and admonition of the Lord, and so he was ultimately responsible for what they did.

The two daughters, in turn, tried to justify their actions by claiming that their father was the only man left alive and that they simply wanted to keep the family name going by producing offspring. But their motive, however worthy, doesn't remove their guilt. The result was the birth of two boys, one through each daughter: (1) a son named *Moab*, traditionally thought to mean "from [my] father," who became the ancestor of the Moabites; and (2) a son named *Ben-ammi*, which means "son of my kinsman," who became the ancestor of the Ammonites (see also Deut. 2:9,19).

How tragic that Lot's seven downward steps led eventually to the founding of two nations who were to become bitter enemies of the descendants of his uncle Abraham!

Abimelech and Sarah—20:1-18

Genesis 20:1-18 and 26:6-11 are often considered to be simply duplicates or alternates of the story told in 12:10-20.[1] But we should observe that there are differences between the accounts as well as similarities between them. Also, there is no reason why Abraham shouldn't try again (20:1-18) what had gained him so much wealth the first time (12:10-20). And there is likewise no reason why his son, Isaac, shouldn't do (26:6-11) what had worked twice for his father!

Abraham and Sarah left the Dead Sea region and took a trip westward into the Negev. They eventually stopped for a while in Gerar, a town located roughly halfway between Gaza and Beersheba. Once again, in order to save his own life, Abraham pretended that Sarah was his sister. She was therefore taken to the palace of Abimelech, the ruler of Gerar.

In a dream, God told Abimelech that he was as good as dead because he had taken another man's wife to become one of the women in his harem. God was determined not only to preserve the sanctity of marriage but also the purity of the covenant line (Isaac had not yet been born to Sarah).

At the same time, God also respected Abimelech's protestations of innocence. After all, he had not yet so much as touched Sarah, and in any event he didn't know she was Abraham's wife. So the Lord told Abimelech to release Sarah to Abraham, who, as a prophet (Gen. 20:7; see also Ps. 105:15), would intercede for Abimelech's life. How intricate are the ways of God, and how marvelous is His grace: He instructed the deceiver to pray for the deceived!

Like the pharaoh before him (Gen. 12:18,19), Abimelech summoned Abraham, confronted him with the lie he had told, and asked him why he did it. We must not miss the irony of Abraham's reply: "Because I thought, surely there is no fear of God in this place" (20:11)! Obviously, Abimelech feared God more than Abraham did at this point! The Spirit of the Lord moves where He will, and often God's people are too hasty in making judgments about where He can and cannot work.

Abraham then explained—or, rather, gave the excuse—that Sarah *was* his sister; well, at least she was his half-sister! Abraham and Sarah had been born of the same father, but not of the same mother (20:12). They may have been offspring resulting from Terah's polygamy; if so, we have before us yet another demonstration of the evils of having more than one wife.

After Abimelech had given Abraham a substantial gift of animals and servants, he restored Sarah to him and invited him to stay in his territory if he so desired. He also gave Sarah a

47

thousand shekels of silver as proof of her innocence in the whole matter. Then Abraham, perhaps somewhat sheepishly in the light of the circumstances, prayed for the removal of the affliction that had overcome Abimelech and his household because he had taken Sarah into his palace (20:17,18; see also 12:17).

The Birth of Isaac—21:1-34

Even men of God like Abraham may sometimes disappoint us, but God Himself never fails. Always true to His word, He gave Sarah her promised son, Isaac (Gal. 4:28), just as He had said He would (Gen. 21:1,2; see 17:16,21; 18:10,14). Soon after Isaac's birth and in accord with God's command (17:12), a 100-year-old man circumcised his eight-day-old baby boy! Joy reigned in that home (21:6), reflecting the meaning of Isaac's name, "he laughs." (See also 17:17; 18:12-15.)

Since mothers in the ancient Near East nursed their babies for a much longer period of time than modern Western mothers do, Isaac may have been two or even three years old[2] when Abraham prepared a sumptuous feast to celebrate his weaning (21:8). On that occasion Sarah saw Ishmael, who was now in his late teens (see 16:16), at play, and she suddenly realized that he was a potential threat to Isaac's inheritance.

According to the legal practices of that time, she had no genuine cause for worry. The Nuzi documents, to which we have already referred so often in this book, imply that, just as the inheritance rights of a son born to a man and his servant girl take precedence over the rights of an adopted son, so also do the inheritance rights of a son born to a man and his wife take precedence over those of a servant girl's son.[3] To summarize the matter in the context of Abraham's family, just as Ishmael's rights superseded those of Eliezer, so also Isaac's rights would now supersede those of Ishmael.

In another sense, however, we can understand Sarah's fears. After all, Ishmael was much older than Isaac, and that fact may have played a part in her anxiety. In any event, she asked Abraham to drive Hagar and Ishmael out of the house. Such an act would have had the effect of disinheriting Ishmael.

Abraham was displeased at this request (21:11), and perhaps

for more than one reason. He had doubtless come to love Ishmael very much by now. But in addition there was the legal question, once again illuminated by documents from Nuzi. Because of the relatively weak legal status of a servant girl's son, the law protected him by forbidding that he be driven out of the household. Sarah, then, was not within her legal rights by requesting the expulsion of Ishmael.

Nevertheless, God overruled and told Abraham to do as Sarah had asked, because it was Isaac who would carry on Abraham's line and receive his inheritance (21:12). Paul quoted part of this verse to show that it is children of promise, and not children of flesh, who are Abraham's true descendants (Rom. 9:6-8). So just being a physical descendant of Abraham is not a guarantee of also being his spiritual heir, a genuine believer.

The writer of Hebrews also stressed the importance of Genesis 21:12 by relating it to God's command to sacrifice Isaac in Genesis 22 (Heb. 11:17-19). In so doing, he demonstrated the close connection between Genesis 21 and 22 by showing that it was Isaac, the son of promise, the one through whom Abraham's descendants would be named, that God was telling Abraham to slaughter on an altar of sacrifice.

As we have seen, the New Testament recognized the significance of Isaac as the son of promise (Gal. 4:28). But God assured Abraham that Ishmael also would be the ancestor of a powerful nation (Gen. 21:13), just as He had promised Hagar earlier (16:10) and would promise her again (21:18). Because our faith is often weak, God gives us repeated assurances of His loving concern.

And so, for the second time, Hagar was driven out of Abraham's household through Sarah's instigation. This time her teenage son Ishmael accompanied her into the desert. When their water supply ran out, the Lord directed her to a well so the boy wouldn't die of thirst (21:19). Ishmael grew up in the desert of Paran in the Sinai peninsula, and eventually he married an Egyptian girl at his Egyptian mother's request (21:21). As often happens in the Near East today, marriages in those early days were arranged by the parents of the young people involved and not by the young people themselves.

Meanwhile, Abraham and his family had stayed in

Abimelech's territory, the land of Philistia, for some time (21:34). So important did the Philistines become in that part of the world that the entire area was eventually named "Palestine" after them. They didn't arrive there in large numbers until after 1200 B. C. during a time of general political and social ferment in the Near East, but it is not unlikely that smaller settlements of "Philistines" had lived there intermittently in previous centuries.[4] The description in Genesis 21 indicates that their presence in Canaan tended to be peaceful during those early years. Abimelech was impressed by Abraham's obviously close relationship to God, and so he decided he wanted Abraham as an ally rather than as an enemy. Abraham readily accepted Abimelech's offer of friendship (21:22-24).

Genesis 21 closes with an account of Abraham's complaint to Abimelech concerning a well that was owned by Abraham but that had been taken over by Abimelech's servants. The dispute was settled when the two men agreed to "make" (literally, "cut"; see 15:18) a covenant, taking an oath to resolve their differences in a mutually beneficial way. Abimelech accepted seven of Abraham's lambs as a witness to Abraham's ownership of the well. In memory of the event, the place was named *Beersheba*, which means both "well of seven" and "well of the oath." To this very day there is an ancient well in modern Beersheba that is still pointed out as "Abraham's well," but we can't be certain of its authenticity.

Abraham planted a tree in Beersheba in honor of the Lord, who is called here, and here only, *El Olam*, "God Everlasting" (21:33). It is a name that stresses His eternal nature. God's promises and covenants are everlasting, because God Himself is eternal.

Footnotes

1. See, for example, H. H. Rowley, *The Growth of the Old Testament* (New York: Harper Torchbook, 1963), pp. 17, 18.

2. E. A. Speiser, *The Anchor Bible: Genesis* (Garden City: Doubleday & Company, Inc., 1964), p. 155.

3. C. F. Pfeiffer, ed., *The Biblical World* (Grand Rapids: Baker Book House, 1966), p. 423.

4. K. A. Kitchen, *Ancient Orient and Old Testament* (Chicago: Inter-Varsity Press, 1966), pp. 80, 81.

5

ABRAHAM:
His Trial
Genesis 22:1—23:20

The twin covenant promises of descendants and land, given by God to His friend Abraham, seemed to be well on their way to fulfillment.

Isaac had now been born and weaned. He had therefore successfully weathered the most critical period of his early life. All other things being equal, he should have had very little trouble growing up to be a fine young man in the environment of a loving home.

Abraham had now settled down in the land of Canaan. He had come to know the land intimately and had been living there with his family for quite some time.

But suddenly each of the two promises—the promise of descendants, and the promise of land—met an obstacle designed to test Abraham's faith. And the first obstacle tested it almost to the breaking point.

At Moriah—22:1-24

If I were asked to choose the three most important chapters in the story of Abraham's life, I would select Genesis 12, telling us of his call; Genesis 15, describing his conversion and the covenant God made with him; and Genesis 22, detailing the most severe test that God ever put him through.

If I were then asked to choose the most important chapter among these three, I would find it very difficult to do so. But on balance I think I would have to select Genesis 22, because in it Abraham faced the most profound spiritual crisis of his entire life.

A long time had elapsed (Gen. 21:34), and Isaac was no longer a small child. Ties of mutual love and respect had had a chance to grow and develop between Abraham and his son. So, from God's standpoint, the time was now ripe to "test" Abraham (22:1).

That crucial verb is capable of more than one translation, as the various English versions demonstrate. But in this context it is better to render it "prove" (*ASV*) or "test" (*NASB, RSV*) than "tempt" (*KJV*), since God never tempts anyone (Jas. 1:13). We can be tempted by Satan (1 Cor. 7:5) or by our own desires and lusts (Jas. 1:14), but we can never be tempted by God.

There are two important differences between temptation and testing that we need to keep in mind. One has to do with their subject and the other with their object. It is Satan who tempts us, but it is God who tests us. And Satan tempts us in order to destroy us (1 Pet. 5:8; Jas. 1:15; Rom. 6:23), but God tests us in order to strengthen us (Exod. 20:20; Deut. 8:2). When God tests you, it is only because He wants "to do good for you in the end" (Deut. 8:16).

God knows His people intimately, so when He came to test Abraham He called him by name. Abraham answered with the response of the servant: "Here I am" (Gen. 22:1). It was a response that would be echoed by Joseph (to his father Jacob, in this case; 37:13), Samuel (1 Sam. 3:4,6,8), Isaiah (Isa. 6:8), and many others, right down to our own time. Sensitive and devout people are still hearing and responding to God's call today.

God said to Abraham (Gen. 22:2), "Take now your *son*."

"But which one, Lord?" Abraham may have thought. "After all, I have two sons, Ishmael and Isaac."

"Your *only* son."

"That's still ambiguous, Lord. I need more specific directions than *that*!"

"*Whom you love.*"

"But Lord, I love *both* my sons."

"*Isaac!*"

"Thank you, Lord! Now I know exactly who you mean. And what shall I do after I go and get Isaac? Is it something that will further your will and purpose for his life?"

"Go to the land of Moriah."

"A little vacation for us! Fine! And then what?"

"*Offer him there as a burnt offering on one of the mountains of which I will tell you!*"

At that point, Abraham must have nearly fainted, overcome by disbelief. Had he heard God correctly? Was Isaac, the son of promise, finally born, finally grown into vigorous young manhood, now going to die? Was the glorious promise of God (Gen. 15:4) now going to be nullified? Abraham's faith was being tested severely!

In telling Abraham to go and get one of his sons, our loving God broke the news to him gently, withholding Isaac's name till the very end. At the same time, God used terms that were calculated to make Abraham fully aware of the high price He was asking him to pay: "Take . . . your *only* son, *whom you love*" (italics added).

But God never asks us to do something He Himself is unwilling to do. We need to remember that God, also, gave His one and only Son (John 3:16; 1 John 4:9; Acts 2:23) as a once-for-all sacrifice (Heb. 9:28) for the sins of the world (1 John 4:14).

Abraham surely did not yet know that God was going to do that, however. So his response of prompt obedience was all the more remarkable: he got up "early in the morning" (Gen. 22:3) to begin the journey. If ever a man was tempted to procrastinate, Abraham could easily have been such a man that day! But prompt and unquestioning eagerness to do the will of God was one of Abraham's admirable characteristics, as we have already seen (12:4; 17:23; 21:14).

53

(KJ) Gen. 22:2 "And he said, Take now thy son, thine
only son Isaac, whom thou lovest —"

His destination was Moriah (22:2), a place mentioned elsewhere only in 2 Chronicles 3:1. There it is called "Mount Moriah"; it was the site on which Solomon's temple in Jerusalem was eventually built. The temple was destroyed in 586 B. C. by the Babylonians, and Zerubbabel's temple was built on or near the same location 70 years later. That temple, in turn, was strengthened and refurbished by Herod the Great. It stood proudly until its destruction by the Romans in A. D. 70. Today the site is occupied by the Dome of the Rock, an impressive Muslim mosque constructed there in A. D. 691. During the centuries that the Israelites controlled the area, untold thousands of animal sacrifices were offered to God there—but perhaps none quite so unusual as the one Abraham would offer!

Abraham set out for Moriah accompanied by two of his men, a donkey, and, of course, his son Isaac. When they were almost to their destination, Abraham told the men to wait while he and Isaac went on ahead. He said to them, "We will worship and return to you" (Gen. 22:5).

The text clearly states that Abraham told his men that both he and Isaac would come back to them after he and his son had concluded their ceremony of worship. Was Abraham just trying to prop up his own courage? Or was he engaging in wishful thinking? Or was he trying to lead Isaac and the men off the track, to keep them from learning of his true intentions? Or did he already know that God was somehow going to save Isaac's life?

Hebrews 11:17-19 provides us with some helpful comments at this point. Abraham, after all, was a man of faith. He had never seen a resurrection before, but he believed that God was able to perform one if He wanted to do so. And, in a figurative sense, that's exactly what God did!

So Abraham's faith was faith in the ultimate, faith in resurrection from the dead, faith in the greatest miracle of all. This is why Paul could affirm that Abraham's faith in God was of the same quality and calibre as the believer's faith in the resurrection of Christ (Rom. 4:16-25). The outcome of Isaac's near sacrifice was a figurative resurrection (Heb. 11:17-19); the outcome of Jesus' finished sacrifice for our sakes was a literal, historical resurrection (Acts 2:24; 10:40-42; 17:31).

But we're getting a bit ahead of our story. Abraham took wood for the burnt offering and laid it on his son (Gen. 22:6). Are we justified in seeing in that wood a symbol of our sin (Isa. 53:6)? Or are we justified in seeing in it a symbol of the cross of Christ (John 19:17; see also Gen. 22:9)? Perhaps so. At any rate, the burden was placed on Isaac by someone else; it was not of his own doing, even though he voluntarily accepted it.

Abraham escorted Isaac, as it were, to the place of sacrifice. We are told twice that "the two of them walked on together" (Gen. 22:6,8). In a spiritual sense, God the Father and God the Son walked the long road together to Calvary, to the place of sacrifice.

The seven last statements of Jesus on the cross allow us to catch a glimpse of the depth of that relationship. In the first statement, Jesus addressed God as "Father" (Luke 23:34). By the time of the fourth and central statement, the unspeakable suffering of Jesus had strained His relationship to His heavenly Father, and He cried out with a loud voice, "My God, My God" (Matt. 27:46). But the seventh and final statement reflects the close and intimate fellowship they normally enjoyed, for Jesus addressed God once again as "Father" (Luke 23:46).

In the human realm as well, when father and son are at their God-ordained best, their mutual relationship of love and respect can only be strained; it can never be broken.

With the natural curiosity of a boy, Isaac asked Abraham, "Where is the lamb for the burnt offering?" (Gen. 22:7). Abraham, not knowing but believing, answered that God Himself would provide the lamb at the proper time (22:8). At a deeper spiritual level, Isaac was asking his question for all humanity in every age. Every man and woman, every boy and girl in the world today needs to hear John the Baptist's ultimate answer to that question as he introduced Jesus Christ to the people of his time: "Behold, the Lamb of God who takes away the sin of the world!" (John 1:29).

After Abraham had built an altar of sacrifice, Isaac submitted to his father as he tied him up and laid him on the altar on top of the wood (Gen. 22:9). Similarly, Jesus submitted to His role of being the Son under obedience to His Father (Heb. 5:8).

At this point, our story reaches its climax. When Abraham

picked up a knife in order to kill his son, the angel of the Lord shouted from heaven, "Abraham, Abraham!" God had already spoken Abraham's name earlier, but not in this duplicated form (Gen. 22:1). When God repeats the name of a person as He calls him, a situation of urgency is indicated, as with Jacob (46:2), Samuel (1 Sam. 3:10), Saul of Tarsus (Acts 9:4) and others. In Abraham's case, hearing his name shouted twice stopped the downward plunge of the knife!

The angel told Abraham not to harm the boy. Abraham had proved that he feared God, because he had not withheld his only son, Isaac, from Him. His willingness to sacrifice Isaac was clear proof of His deep and abiding faith in God. James saw in it an excellent example of how true faith must be activated and completed by works (Jas. 2:21, 22).

Perhaps a comment is in order about Abraham's "fear" of God (Gen. 22:12). To "fear" God in contexts like this is not so much to "be afraid of" Him or to "dread" Him as it is to "respect" or "revere" Him. It is in this latter sense that the "fear" of the Lord is the beginning of wisdom and knowledge (Prov. 9:10; 1:7). The stock phrase, "fear of the LORD," in the Old Testament is practically a synonym for "true religion." And in the mind of the ancient Israelite, fearing the Lord included loving Him and trusting Him (see especially Deut. 10:12).

True to His promise as Abraham had perceived it by faith (Gen. 22:8), God provided a sacrificial animal by calling Abraham's attention to a ram caught by its horns in a nearby thicket. In gratitude for God's goodness, Abraham named the place "The LORD provides" (22:14; traditionally, *Jehovah-jireh*).

When Abraham sacrificed the ram, he offered it up "in the place of" his son (22:13). This is another clear example of the important biblical doctrine known as substitutionary sacrifice. People of other nations in those early days sometimes offered up human beings as sacrifices to their various gods. But human sacrifice was absolutely forbidden by God to the Israelite, and for obvious reasons. This meant that the sacrificial system God instituted for Israel depended exclusively on substitute sacrifices, usually animals but in some cases plant or plant products. In fact, the whole sacrificial system of the Old Testament is thoroughly infused with the principle of the substitution of one life for another.

Jesus Christ died for our sins, in order to reconcile us to God (2 Cor. 5:17-21). He atoned for our sins, because there is no way that we could atone for them ourselves. Theologians often refer to this process as "substitutionary atonement." The phrase simply means that Christ died in our place so that our sins could be forgiven. Why did Jesus Christ come to this earth? Mark 10:45 tells us: He came to give His life as a ransom "for" (literally, "in the place of") many.

After Abraham had sacrificed the ram as a burnt offering, the angel of the Lord called to him a second time from heaven. He told him that the Lord would indeed bless him and multiply his descendants, promises that were very familiar to Abraham by now (see, for example, Gen. 12:2; 13:16; 17:6). The Lord took an oath to that effect in His own name (22:16), because there is no greater name by which He can swear (Heb. 6:13-15).

Abraham's descendants would not only be as numerous as the stars visible in the sky with the naked eye and numbering in the thousands, as promised earlier (Gen. 15:5), more than that, they would be as numerous as the grains of sand along the seashore, a number so huge it boggles the mind (22:17; see also Heb. 11:12).

His descendants would also occupy the city gates of their enemies (Gen. 22:17), which was tantamount to occupying the cities themselves since controlling the gate was the key to controlling the city. (The gateway of a city was also its most important area in the judicial sphere as well, because that's where legal matters were ordinarily debated and decided; see Ruth 4:1-12.) This promise was later renewed to Rebekah (Gen. 24:60), who was to become Isaac's wife (24:67).

God told Abraham these blessings would take place "because you have obeyed My voice" (22:18). He had not withheld his son, his only son Isaac, his most precious possession, from Him (22:12,16). The parallel between Abraham's devotion and God's love is unmistakable: as Abraham gave to God everything he had, so also God Himself "did not spare His own Son, but delivered Him up for us all" (Rom. 8:32). What amazing grace!

After his mountaintop experience at Moriah, Abraham and his companions went back to Beersheba (Gen. 22:19), where he had lived for a while some time earlier (21:33, 34). His spiritual pilgrimage to the place of sacrifice was a memory that he would treasure forever, but for now he found it necessary to return to his former home and occupation.

Genesis 22 closes with the happy news that Abraham's brother Nahor had become the father of twelve sons. They would later become the ancestors of 12 Aramean (22:21) tribes in their own right.

This brief section describing Nahor's family and including a list of strange names is similar to what Bernard Ramm in another connection has delightfully dubbed "connective tissue."[1] Of only modest interest in itself, it nevertheless serves at least one useful purpose for every reader by giving him an opportunity to catch his breath before plunging into the next chapter of our fast-moving Genesis story.

At Machpelah—23:1-20

In due course, Abraham's wife Sarah died at the age of 127 years (23:1). Her death occurred in Hebron, where the family was living at the time. Hebron was known as *Kiriath-arba* (literally, "the town of Arba") in those days. Arba was the most prominent member of one of the tribes living in the Hebron area (Josh. 14:15). Hebron was also known as Mamre (see Gen. 13:18; 23:19; and especially 35:27), perhaps in memory of one of Abraham's old Amorite friends and allies (14:13,24).

Abraham had always been a dutiful and loving husband. So it was to be expected that he would mourn the loss of his wife, who had shared so much anxiety and grief with him (23:2).

During much of the patriarchal period, the Egyptians and the Hittites jockeyed for domination over certain sections of Palestine. The Egyptians were more numerous but the Hittites had superior weaponry, so standoffs frequently resulted.

At the time of Sarah's death, however, the Hittites were apparently in control of the Hebron area. So Abraham found it necessary to negotiate with the Hittites for a gravesite in which to bury his deceased wife.

The burial plot would be used first for Sarah and later for Abraham himself as well as for other patriarchs and their wives (23:9; 25:8,9; 35:29; 49:28-33). It was known as the cave of

Machpelah. The traditional tombs of Abraham and Sarah, Isaac and Rebekah, and Jacob and Leah are located to this very day deep beneath the Mosque of Abraham, a Muslim shrine in Hebron. Because the mosque is a Muslim holy place, modern visitors cannot go beneath it to see the tomb area itself but must content themselves with seeing the memorial sarcophagi located on an upper level.

When Abraham began his discussion with the Hittites preparatory to negotiating with them for the purchase of the cave, he openly admitted that he was "a stranger and a sojourner" among them (23:4). These were titles that the patriarchs and their descendants were fond of using when referring to themselves (see, for example, David's prayer in 1 Chron. 29:15; see also Ps. 39:12). Hebrews 11:9,13 characterizes the patriarchs as aliens, as strangers, as exiles. While on this earth, they pitched their tents in various places, usually living in the most temporary of dwellings. Nevertheless, they looked forward to living in a city with real foundations, whose architect and builder would be God Himself (Heb. 11:10).

We, too, are in a sense strangers and pilgrims on this planet. While in no way neglecting our duties as good citizens and good neighbors, we nevertheless need to remember that our real and ultimate citizenship is in heaven (Phil. 3:20). Like the patriarchs, we have no lasting city here; we must look forward to the city yet to come (Heb. 13:14).

Owning no land of his own, Abraham was forced to buy a gravesite for Sarah. Genesis 23:3-16 is a classic account of the way in which bargaining was and still is often carried on in the Near East. The verb "give" also meant "sell" in ancient Hebrew, so it occupies a prominent place in the story (Gen. 23:4,9,11,13).

Abraham, the would-be purchaser, bowed down to the Hittites more than once (23:7,12). He needed some land, and so he wanted to be in their good graces. For their part, the Hittites politely offered him the choicest land they had, and apparently at no cost, or at least without mentioning any cost (23:6,11). It's quite clear, however, that they had an eventual selling price in mind (23:15)!

The story is told graphically and tersely. It may even be that not all of the details of the bargaining process are given to us here. But finally Abraham and the Hittites arrived at the mutually agreeable price of 400 shekels of silver at the current market value (23:16). (The shekel during the patriarchal period was a weight, not a coin. Coinage was not invented until hundreds of years later.)

The price of that piece of property was probably just as exorbitant for Abraham's time as the 17-shekel price for a plot of ground in Anathoth was cheap in Jeremiah's time (Jer. 32:9). But Abraham, of course, was in no position to bargain. His need was desperate and he was a stranger, so the Hittites exploited him. The transaction took place at the city gate in the presence of witnesses (23:18). As we noted earlier (see 22:17), the gateway of a city was often the locale for legal transactions of various kinds in ancient times (see especially Ruth 4:11).

What we would call the legal sections of Genesis 23 are written with unusual care. They contain many intentional repetitions and duplications, because they describe an important transaction. Like modern legal documents, they avoid misunderstanding if at all possible.

Recent studies of ancient Hittite law have made it quite likely that Abraham was not interested in buying the entire field in which the cave of Machpelah was located, but only the immediate area around the cave itself. To have bought the whole field would have made Abraham responsible for certain feudal obligations in the society of that time. He therefore may have been requesting only "the end" of the field where the cave was situated (23:9). The Hittites, however, wanting to be completely free of the obligations mentioned, held out for the sale of the whole field, including "all the trees which were in the field" (23:17).[2]

At any rate, the Hittites proved to be very shrewd bargainers, and they clearly took advantage of Abraham's desperate situation. Modern parallels are evident everywhere. Consumer advocacy and other similar groups continually warn us to buy burial plots and learn the various costs involved in funeral arrangements before death occurs in the family. Only by being prepared in advance can we avoid the possibility of being swindled during a time of grief and bereavement.

Having purchased the field, Abraham finally owned a small

part of the promised land. But he had had to pay for it with hard-earned silver, and the occasion for its purchase was the death of his dearly loved wife Sarah.

Abraham's faith in God's promises was being sternly tested once again!

Footnotes

1. B. L. Ramm, *His Way Out* (Glendale: Regal Books, 1974), pp. 52, 53.
2. See M. R. Lehmann in *Bulletin of the American Schools of Oriental Research* 129 (February 1953), pp. 15-18.

6

ABRAHAM:
His Last Days
Genesis 24:1—25:18

By now, Abraham had become an old man. He decided to make good use of his "golden years" by getting his house in order.

For one thing, he wanted to be sure that his son Isaac married the right girl. In accord with God's promise, Isaac would perpetuate Abraham's name and continue his line, so Abraham was determined to find the perfect mate for his son.

As we observed earlier (see Gen. 21:21), it was the parents who chose mates for their sons and daughters in those days, a practice still followed today in many parts of the Near East. And because of the importance of cementing clan and family relationships, the best marriages of all were considered to be those contracted within one's own tribe rather than with members of another tribe.

Abraham Seeks a Wife for Isaac—24:1-67

The Lord's blessing had followed Abraham throughout his entire life (24:1), and he now wanted that blessing to fall on his son Isaac as well.

He put his oldest servant (perhaps Eliezer of Damascus; see 15:2) in charge of finding a suitable bride for Isaac. To impress the servant with the importance of his mission, Abraham made him take a solemn oath while placing his hand under Abraham's thigh (24:2, 3). The servant was required to put his hand near Abraham's organ of reproduction because the oath was related to the continuation of Abraham's line through Isaac. Years later, Jacob would make Joseph take an oath in a similar way (see 47:29).

Abraham asked his servant to take the oath in the name of "the LORD, the God of heaven and the God of earth" (24:3). That name is majestic indeed; it is reminiscent of the one invoked in Abraham's memorable meeting with Melchizedek so many years before (14:19,22).

The servant was told to find a bride for Isaac, but not from among the girls of Canaan. He was to get her from Abraham's homeland, Mesopotamia, because that's where Abraham's relatives were living. If the chosen bride should refuse to leave Mesopotamia and return to Canaan with the servant, he was not to take Isaac to where she was. In such a case, the servant would be free of the oath he had taken. Abraham's descendants were to live in Canaan, the promised land, not in Mesopotamia, and Abraham had the faith to believe that the girl of God's choice would readily agree to return to Canaan with the servant.

After he had loaded "a variety of good things" (24:10) on ten of Abraham's camels (of which Abraham had a large number; see 12:16), the servant started out from Canaan, taking a few men along with him as companions and aides (see 24:32). Their destination was the city of Nahor near Haran (see 11:32). Like Haran, Nahor was located in *Aram-naharaim*, which means "Aram of the two rivers"—referring to the Tigris and Euphrates Rivers; it was the Hebrew name for the northern portion of what the Greeks would later call *Mesopotamia*, literally, "between the [Tigris and Euphrates] rivers." The men arrived outside Nahor one evening at the coolest time of the day, the time when women normally came out to the town well to get water for their household needs (24:11). Such a scene forms a stark contrast to the otherwise similar picture drawn for us in John 4. There a Samaritan woman, much married and living in sin (and therefore ostracized; John 4:17, 18), found it necessary to go to the well outside her town at "about the sixth hour" (4:6, 7). Since the

63

ancient Near Eastern day was thought of as beginning at about what would correspond to our 6:00 a.m., the woman of Samaria was forced by community pressure to get her water supply at around high noon—the hottest time of the day!

Abraham's servant had apparently learned many lessons from his master. Like Abraham (Gen. 15:8), he too looked for a sign from God to validate his mission. He prayed that God would help him identify the girl He had chosen for Isaac. He prayed that it would be the first girl who would not only offer him a drink of water but would also offer to water his camels.

Prayer in such situations is commendable. When we are in need of divine guidance, prayer should be our first activity rather than our last resort. Our faithful God is always ready to open the storehouse of His blessing, and prayer is often the key that unlocks the storehouse door.

In the case of Abraham's servant, his simple faith in God's providence was not ill-founded. He appealed to the intimate, covenant relationship that existed between Abraham and God (24:14). The Lord had bound Himself in a pact of "lovingkindness" to his master Abraham. The servant rightly felt that such a pact was reason enough for the Lord to give him success on his important mission.

And God was quick to answer that earnest request! Before the servant had even finished praying, a beautiful virgin girl came to the well and began to fulfill the conditions of his prayer. God is not slow in responding to our pleas. Even before we conclude our prayers, His answer is already on the way.

But the servant wanted to be absolutely sure that what he had just seen wouldn't turn out to be a false alarm. So, in silence, he watched the girl finish the task of watering his camels (24:21).

He then gave her a gold nose-ring (24:22; see 24:47) and two gold bracelets as gifts. He asked her whose daughter she was, and also whether there would be room on her father's estate for him, his companions, and his animals to spend the night there.

When she told him that she was Nahor's granddaughter and that there was indeed plenty of room, the servant bowed his head in worship and prayer. He now knew that God had made his journey successful by leading him to the right place (24:26, 27).

The girl, whose name was Rebekah (24:15, 29), ran to her

house to break the news that a camel caravan had been sent to Nahor by their relative Abraham. Her brother Laban, in turn, ran out to the well to invite the servant into the house and give him a royal welcome. But the servant refused to eat the food that was set before him until he had given a full account of his errand (24:33).

Genesis 24 is the longest chapter in the book of Genesis. This is partly because the servant, at this point in the chapter, now repeated the whole story of his mission (24:34-49), a story that we have already read. But the repetition is not monotonous or slavish. It contains a few elegant variations, as well as a few additional details.

Also, Genesis 24 as a whole is an excellent example of the ancient storyteller's art. In those days people enjoyed repetition—in fact, they preferred it—as they listened to tales or read them. Such repetition, in whole or in part, helped to fix the story in their memories.

In one sense Genesis 24, in spite of its length, comes to a rather abrupt conclusion. Rebekah's brother Laban and her father Bethuel agreed, after hearing the servant's story, to allow Rebekah to leave with him. They believed that it was the Lord's will (24:50) for her to do so, and they could easily have echoed a later psalmist's shout of wonder: "It is marvelous in our eyes" (Ps.118:23). They also realized, as did Gamaliel the Pharisee two thousand years later (Acts 5:38, 39), that if a matter originates with God and is therefore God's will, we had better do nothing to oppose it or Him.

Bethuel's and Laban's consent to allow Rebekah to leave caused Abraham's servant to again worship the Lord in gratitude (Gen. 24:52). He must have been an unusually godly man to display so frequently his dependence on the Lord in all matters. Abraham had doubtless taught him well and had been a good example to him.

After a good night's rest, however, Rebekah's relatives had second thoughts about allowing her to leave home so quickly. So they requested that she be permitted to remain in Mesopotamia for ten days or so. It is understandable that they would want to keep her with them as long as possible, since Canaan was a long distance away and they might never see her again.

But the servant wanted to be on his way, because God had made his journey successful up to this point and he now wanted to see it through to its conclusion. So Rebekah was asked her opinion on the matter, and she immediately agreed to leave right away (24:58). Her relatives then gave her a blessing of their own (24:60; for a similar blessing, see 22:17) and sent her off together with her nurse (24:59), whose name was Deborah (see 35:8), and her servant girls (24:61). And so they started out on their long journey to Canaan.

On the evening of their arrival in the Negev in the southern part of the promised land, Isaac happened to be out walking in the fields. He had recently come from Beer-lahai-roi, the well where the angel of the Lord had met Hagar (16:14) and where Isaac himself would settle down after his father's death (25:11).

When Rebekah saw Isaac approaching and found out who he was, she covered herself with her veil, an act of modesty as well as a sign of her forthcoming marriage. After the servant had told Isaac the whole story, Isaac brought Rebekah into his deceased mother's tent and she became his wife. For Isaac, married life began at forty (25:20)!

In summary, from Genesis 24 we can learn a great deal about how marriages were contracted in ancient times in that part of the world. By and large, it was the parents that decided who their sons and daughters would marry. Sometimes the arrangements were made through an intermediary, such as a trusted servant. The best marriages were considered those contracted within one's own tribe rather than with a member of another tribe. To marry one's cousin was especially desirable, although such inbreeding often had unfortunate consequences when sickly or even deformed children were born as a result of such unions. A modern example of the fact that this practice is unwise can be found among the present-day Samaritan community in Israel who, until quite recently, have seen their numbers gradually depleted by such marriages. Inbreeding through the course of the centuries has reduced their population to about 500.[1]

Substantial gifts were customarily given by a young man (or his parents) to the bride, as well as to members of her immediate family (24:53). The girl herself remained veiled until after the marriage. It is interesting to note that these two customs have remained in force in a modified form in Western marriages even today.

But details about ancient marriages, however interesting in themselves, are merely incidental to the main point of Genesis 24: an all-loving and all-powerful God was working in and through the lives of all the people involved in the story. An oath was taken in His name; He led Abraham's servant to the right town and the right girl; Rebekah's relatives recognized Him as the one whose will had to be obeyed in the matter; and Rebekah was so impressed by the servant's obviously sincere and honest account of how God had guided him step by step that she accompanied him back to Canaan without hesitation.

As for Isaac himself, it is entirely possible that he, too, had sensed the Lord's guidance in preparing his own heart to welcome Rebekah when she arrived. The traditional interpretation of Genesis 24:63 indicates that he had gone out into the fields to "meditate" that very evening. Unfortunately, we cannot be certain about the meaning of the verb in question, and other translations have been proposed (see, for example, *NASB* margin). But meditation is the kind of spiritual exercise that would have been entirely in character for Isaac, because many years later he would pray that the Lord would be gracious to Rebekah and allow her to bear children (25:21), and his prayer would be answered. So he may well have been praying and meditating on his wedding night.

If ever a marriage was made in heaven, this one was!

Abraham Marries Keturah—25:1-6

These six verses describe another marriage and its results, but in a much briefer way. The section is perhaps a flashback, since Abraham would have been 140 years old by now if chronological order were demanded.

Strictly speaking, Keturah was Abraham's concubine (1 Chron. 1:32) rather than his wife. The Hebrew word for "wife" in Genesis 25:1 can also just as legitimately be translated "woman." In fact, Abraham had more than one concubine (Gen. 25:6), a matter that we must take into consideration in attempting to understand the sexual morality of that early period of history. The Old Testament nowhere condones concubinage, but at the same time it does not try to gloss over it, even when its principal characters, many of whom were godly men, indulged in it.

There were six Keturite tribes in all, and Medan and Midian were ancestors of two of them (25:2). They in turn were related to Ishmael, Abraham's son through the Egyptian servant girl Hagar. When we take the time to observe these complex relationships, we are then able to explain how the caravanners who later sold Joseph into Egypt can be called "Ishmaelites" (37:25,27,28), "Midianites" (37:28) and "Medanites" (37:36 *NASB* margin) all at the same time (see also Judg. 8:22, 24,26).

After he had given gifts to the sons of his concubines, Abraham sent them all away to their future homes east of the Jordan river (Gen. 25:6). The lion's share of his estate, however, went to Isaac, his firstborn under the law (25:5).

Nuzi contract documents clearly illustrate the so-called "law of primogeniture" in effect in ancient times. That law provided for the transmission of at least a double share of the father's property to the firstborn son upon the father's death (see, for example, Deut. 21:15-17). In other words, the firstborn son was to receive at least twice as large a share of the estate as any other son received. (The wording of Gen. 25:5 indicates that Isaac received far more than the double share to which he was entitled by law!)

The law of primogeniture was universally followed, except in unusual circumstances. A case in point was that of the daughters of Zelophehad. Their father had died without leaving any sons, so they understandably requested title to his estate. When Moses brought their case before the Lord, he was told that the women were indeed entitled to their father's property. In fact, the case became the basis of expanding the laws of inheritance to take care of other contingent situations as well (Num. 27:1-11).

An interesting spiritual application of the terms of the law of primogeniture took place just before Elijah was taken by the Lord. When Elijah gave Elisha the opportunity of making a request of him, Elisha said, "Please, let a double portion of your spirit be upon me" (2 Kings 2:9). In the light of the law of primogeniture, it is clear that Elisha was not asking for twice the spiritual power that Elijah had possessed. He merely wanted Elijah to designate him as his main spiritual heir.

Abraham Dies and Is Buried—25:7-11

"Precious in the sight of the LORD is the death of His godly ones" (Ps.116:15)!

When he was 175 years old, a full century after his departure from Haran (if we interpret the numbers literally), Abraham died at "a ripe old age" (Gen. 25:8), as God had promised he would (15:15). Dying at "a ripe old age" was as much a reference to quality of life as it was to length of life. The phrase is not used, for example, of Ishmael at the time of his death (25:17).

Abraham was buried in the cave of Machpelah near the grave of his beloved wife Sarah. It was "his sons Isaac and Ishmael" who buried him (25:9). The order in which the names of the sons is mentioned is significant, since Ishmael was the older of the two. It underscores the fact that Isaac was recognized as Abraham's firstborn in the eyes of the law and in the eyes of God.

If the sheer number of chapters devoted to his life is any indication, the most important man in the book of Genesis had now passed from the scene. But although gone, he was not forgotten. He would be recalled by future generations of believers as a man of faith and obedience, eventually to be honored by Jew, Christian, and Muslim alike. His towering figure would cast a long and beneficial shadow over the history of his descendants.

As God had promised, Abraham would, indeed, become the "father of a multitude." He would be the revered ancestor of the people of Israel, the chosen people, the people who would make the most lasting impact on the religious history of mankind.

And most significant of all, to both Jew and Gentile Abraham would be remembered as the spiritual father of all who believe.

The Generations of Ishmael—25:12-18

Although a literary unit in its own right, bearing the catch-phrase introduction "These are the generations of . . ." (see chap. 1), this paragraph also serves as an appendix to the story of Abraham's life. It is somewhat anticlimactic, bridging the gap between Abraham's story and Jacob's story. It is essentially a genealogy, another example of "connective tissue" (see 22:20-24). Not particularly noteworthy in itself, it nevertheless performs the useful function of attaching one major part of the Genesis organism to another.

Like Nahor, one of Abraham's brothers (22:20-24), Ishmael became the ancestor of 12 tribes. Many of their names indicate that Arabs were included among their descendants. This fact gives credence to the Arab tradition that Abraham was the ancestor of the Arabs through Ishmael.

Although Genesis 25:18 is rather difficult to translate and interpret, it at least states that Ishmael's descendants settled down in an extensive area east of Egypt and that they tended to be antagonistic toward other tribes (see also 16:12) including, of course, the tribes of Israel. So the Arab-Jewish rivalry that has exploded into open hostility now and then through the centuries had its beginnings among the early descendants of Ishmael and Isaac.

Ishmael's ancestry of twelve tribes was in direct fulfillment of the Lord's promise to Abraham (17:20). Our God, who never changes, can always be depended on to keep His word to us, just as he did to Ishmael through Abraham, who was his father, our spiritual ancestor, and God's friend.

> The God of Abraham praise,
> Who reigns enthroned above;
> Ancient of everlasting days,
> And God of love.
>
> Jehovah, great I AM,
> By earth and heaven confessed;
> I bow and bless the sacred Name,
> Forever blest.
>
> —Daniel ben Judah

Footnote

1. See *Facts About Israel* (Jerusalem: Division of Information, Ministry for Foreign Affairs, 1973), p. 75.

7

JACOB:

His Early Years at Home
Genesis 25:19–27:46

We have now come to a major break in the book of Genesis. It is signalized by the telltale phrase, "These are the generations of . . ." (25:19; see chap. 1). To all intents and purposes, we have left the story of Abraham behind us, although his memory will continue to exercise a strong and beneficial influence over the people and events discussed in the rest of Genesis.

But the life of Abraham's grandson, Jacob, will now occupy our attention for the most part. And, in many respects, the personalities and activities of Jacob and Abraham provide quite a series of contrasts, as we shall see!

Birth and Birthright—25:19-34

After Isaac's marriage to Rebekah (24:67), many years passed, and Rebekah did not become pregnant. In similar situations today, most couples probably go to the doctor's office to find out what's physically or psychologically wrong with the husband or wife. Or they simply wring their hands in despair.

71

But Isaac knew what to do: he prayed to the Lord on his wife's behalf (25:21). His example reminds us that we should pray for things that we desire and that we believe to be in the will of God. Isaac believed that God wanted him to have a son—perhaps because his father had told him about God's promise of many descendants. Since the covenant with Abraham was eternal and unbreakable from God's standpoint (17:7), Isaac decided to take the matter of Rebekah's sterility directly to God Himself. If God couldn't make Rebekah fertile, he reasoned, no one could.

Needless to say, God is a specialist in the art of answering difficult prayers. And He answered Isaac's prayer in a lavish way: Rebekah conceived twin boys (25:24).

The new surge of life inside her must have made Rebekah very happy. But before long the babies began to jostle each other in her womb to the point where she was in such physical distress that she wondered whether pregnancy was really such a desirable experience after all (25:22). Many years later, she would have similar doubts and ask similar questions when one of her boys had married a couple of Hittite girls and she was afraid the other boy would do the same (27:46). Rearing children has never been a simple matter, and the boys in Rebekah's womb would doubtless give their parents more than the usual number of problems as they grew up in that home.

But at some point during her difficult pregnancy, it would seem that the vitality of Rebekah's prayer life matched that of her husband Isaac. She asked the Lord for an explanation of what was happening inside her (25:22). The Lord told her that the boys in her womb would become the ancestors of two nations, and that the older would serve the younger (25:23).

This incident is referred to by Paul in Romans 9:10-12 during a discussion of God's sovereign right to make choices according to His own good pleasure. Paul's description of the scene and his theological understanding of it are worth quoting in full and without comment: "There was Rebekah also, when she had conceived twins by one man, our father Isaac; for though the twins were not yet born, and had not done anything good or bad, in order that God's purpose according to His choice might stand, not because of works, but because of Him who calls, it was said to her, 'The older will serve the younger.' "

And so the younger of Rebekah's twins was chosen by God in preference to the older. This meant, of course, that God's covenant promises to Abraham would be fulfilled through the younger boy.

How often have we seen this to be true throughout biblical history! It seems that God *almost always* chose a younger son in preference to the firstborn male. Perhaps He did this in order to break the hammerlock hold the sacrosanct law of primogeniture had over society in ancient times. But most supremely God did this so that He would be able to demonstrate His sovereign will in defiance of man-made laws and institutions. We observe that most of the great men of the Old Testament—Jacob, Joseph, Judah, Moses and David, for example—were not the firstborn sons in their respective families.

In Rebekah's case, her firstborn son emerged from the womb all red and covered with hair, so he was named *Esau,* which apparently meant "hairy." His twin brother was born immediately afterward with his hand holding firmly onto Esau's heel, so he was named *Jacob,* the "heel-holder" or "supplanter." The same word is used, for example, in Jeremiah 9:4 with the meaning "supplant," A similarly unusual birth of twin boys is described in Genesis 38:27-30.

Isaac was 60 years old when Esau and Jacob were born (25:26), and Abraham was 100 years old at the time of Isaac's birth (21:5). Since Abraham lived to be 175 (25:7), he was still living when Isaac's twin boys were born. It is likely then that he saw and played with Esau and Jacob in their formative years and that he recognized in them the continuing fulfillment of God's promise of many descendants.

Esau would eventually become the ancestor of the Edomites and Jacob of the Israelites. Although the mutual relationships of those tribes should have been brotherly, such was unfortunately not always the case (see Num. 20:14-21; Obad. 9, 10).

As the two boys grew up, striking differences between them soon became evident. Esau was an outdoorsman who loved to hunt, while Jacob tended to be a quiet homebody (Gen. 25:27). Unfortunately, Isaac favored Esau because he thoroughly enjoyed the meat that Esau brought in from the hunt, while Rebekah preferred Jacob's company, probably because he provided companionship for her and maybe even assisted with the household chores.

Parental favoritism is never a good thing, and yet all of us know of homes in which one child is favored over the others. Such partiality can easily destroy not only the children who are comparatively neglected but also the pampered one as well. There is no place in the Christian home for the rivalry and bitterness that inevitably result from parental favoritism toward one or more of the children.

While it is certainly true that some children are just naturally more lovable than others, the beauty of the less lovable child will never be brought out or nurtured by neglecting him. The temptation to be partial may sternly test the character of any parent. But unless we resist that temptation, we will make it very difficult for some of our children to develop their abilities and capacities to the fullest. Parental favoritism certainly turned out to be bad in the case of Esau and Jacob, as we shall see in our study of Genesis 27.

Because he spent a lot of time at home, Jacob became a good cook. One day when Jacob had made a pot of vegetable stew, Esau came in from the hunt. He was famished, so he asked Jacob for a helping of that reddish-colored stew. (The memorable incident gave him the nickname *Edom,* "Red," 25:30; we recall also that he had been red when he emerged from his mother's womb, 25:25.)

Jacob readily agreed to give Esau some stew if he was willing to trade his birthright for it. That was hardly a bargain offer for Esau, since by definition the birthright belonged only to the firstborn son and guaranteed him at least twice as much inheritance from his father's estate as any of his brothers could expect to receive (Deut. 21:17).

But Esau thought he was starving to death (Gen. 25:32). Feeling that his birthright was of no use to him in such circumstances, he agreed on oath to sell it to Jacob in exchange for the stew.

The legality of such a sale is now known to have been a part of ancient life, as contract documents from Nuzi demonstrate.[1] But it is nevertheless incredible that Esau entered into such a transaction, with all of its ramifications in the light of the

Abrahamic covenant. His decision shows how immoral and godless he was, according to the evaluation of Hebrews 12:16, the author of which was amazed at Esau's willingness to sell his own birthright "for a single meal."

Genesis 25:34 also observes that Esau, in so doing, "despised" his birthright. The story as a whole serves as an example of the dangers of materialism, of allowing one's appetites to become the most important things in life.

Both men, of course, were in the wrong. Jacob sinned by taking advantage of Esau during a moment of weakness. And Esau sinned by falling for Jacob's ridiculous offer and by succumbing to his own hunger pangs.

But Esau's sin was the greater of the two, and it would have far-reaching consequences later on. see also p. 101

Miscellaneous Episodes—26:1-35

The inspired writer's attention shifted back to Isaac in Genesis 26, and we can now see how lackluster was Isaac's personality and how very ordinary were his activities. Isaac's character strikes us as being quite bland and passive in comparison to his father Abraham's. He had a hard act to follow, of course; he was destined to live in the shadow of his father's greatness. But he was so unimaginative that he did almost nothing original or on his own. In fact, just about his only claim to fame is his longevity: he lived to be 180 years of age (35:28), five years longer than the age Abraham was able to reach!

Famine descended on the land of Canaan (26:1), just as it had in the days of Abraham (12:10). In this case, Isaac and Rebekah did not go all the way down to Egypt, as Abraham and Sarah had done. The Lord appeared to Isaac (26:2), as He had so many times before to Abraham, and specifically told him and Rebekah not to go to Egypt. He told them instead to go to Gerar, where Abraham and Sarah had gone after the destruction of Sodom and Gomorrah. There, in the land of the Philistines, God would prosper Isaac and confirm the Abrahamic covenant to and through him. He would do this because of Abraham's obedience, a fact that once again emphasizes the conditional nature of those covenant blessings (26:5).

How gracious God is! Memories of past divine favor and love

seem to fade so quickly, but when they do God is always ready and able to give His children continued reassurances of His concern and reminders of His promises.

The king of the Philistines at that time was Abimelech (26:1). He was probably the son, or even the grandson, of the Abimelech who ruled over Gerar in Abraham's time (20:2). It was not unusual in those days for kings to adopt the names of their predecessors, whether recent or remote—a practice that has continued right down to the present.

Isaac lied to his Abimelech—just as Abraham had lied to the earlier one. Isaac did so for the same reason Abraham had done so. And the results were also the same: the lie was discovered, and Isaac was rebuked by a pagan king. What a sad example of "like father, like son"!

And yet, so amazing is God's grace that, in spite of everything, He blessed Isaac (26:12)! His crops were so bountiful and his flocks became so huge that Abimelech felt it necessary to expel him from Philistia. Isaac was becoming far too wealthy and powerful for Abimelech (26:16). When God decides to do so, He blesses His children in spite of themselves because His grace is greater than their sin.

Driven away from Gerar by Abimelech, Isaac set up camp in a nearby ravine. There he emptied the debris out of some wells that had been dug originally by Abraham and later plugged up by the Philistines. The redug wells did not supply Isaac's family and flocks with enough water, however, so his servants dug another well. But the herdsmen of Gerar quarreled with Isaac's herdsmen and claimed the water from that well for themselves, so it was named *Esek,* which means "quarrel." When Isaac's servants dug another well, it too became a bone of contention, so it was named *Sitnah* ("hostility"). Finally Isaac moved some distance away and had another well dug. This time no one quarreled over it, so it was named *Rehoboth* ("Plenty of room").

Eventually Isaac left the region of Gerar entirely and went to Beersheba. There the Lord appeared to him again and said to him, "Do not fear, for I am with you" (26:24). God's promise to be with us is repeated often in the Bible (see, for example, Gen. 26:3; 28:15; 31:3; Matt. 28:20; Acts 18:10). When we are at our spiritual best, we want that kind of relationship with Him. And

He desires such fellowship with us also. When Jesus appointed His 12 disciples, the first reason given for that appointment was "that they might be with Him" (Mark 3:14). The joy of love is to be with those we love.

The Lord told Isaac that His presence with him would enable him to live without fear (Gen. 26:24). Freedom from fear, an age-long hope of people everywhere from time immemorial, was one of the late Franklin D. Roosevelt's highly publicized "Four Freedoms." Isaac was told that true freedom from fear comes only in having a personal relationship with God. For today's believer, such a relationship can be found only in Jesus Christ (John 14:1-6).

At Beersheba, Isaac was again reminded of God's promises to Abraham, and in gratitude for the Lord's faithfulness he built an altar there. Isaac's servants, meanwhile, dug another well (Gen. 26:25), which was named *Shibah* ("oath," 26:33) because of a covenant signed there between Abimelech and Isaac (26:26-31). Even though Abimelech had earlier sent Isaac away from Philistia, he recognized that God was with him and therefore wanted him as a friend rather than an enemy.

Beersheba ("well of the oath") had been given its name originally because of a significant event in the life of Abraham that had occurred there (21:25-31). Now its name was confirmed because of a similar event in Isaac's life. This is only one of many instances in Genesis 26 demonstrating that Isaac essentially repeated what his father had done rather than striking out in new directions. Living in the shadow of Abraham's greatness made it difficult for Isaac to assert his own originality and independence.

As Isaac had married at forty years of age (25:20), so did his son Esau (26:34). But while Isaac had married one Aramean girl and had done so according to God's specific will, Esau married two Hittite girls who made life miserable for his parents and who also made Rebekah determined not to allow Jacob to make the same mistake (26:34,35; 27:46).

Blessing for Jacob and Esau—27:1-46

Before the rise of modern medicine, blindness and near blindness were common afflictions of elderly people (see Gen. 48:10). This is why Moses' good vision at the end of his life was

77

so noteworthy (Deut. 34:7). Isaac's weak vision in his old age forms the backdrop of Genesis 27.

Isaac didn't know that Esau had sold his birthright to Jacob, so he made preparations to bless his firstborn son Esau (27:1-4). Possession of the birthright was tantamount to receiving the blessing of the firstborn (see Heb. 12:16,17), even though Esau would later try to separate the two (Gen. 27:31-38).

Isaac told Esau to go out and hunt some game and then to prepare a tasty meal for him, so that after Isaac had eaten he could bless him. Meanwhile Rebekah, who had been eavesdropping on the conversation, went and told Jacob about it. She then instructed him to go and get two young goats which she would prepare into a tasty meal. The full tragedy of this instance of parental favoritism (see 25:28) unfolds bit by bit as the story proceeds.

Emphasized throughout the account is the phrase "such as [Isaac] loves" (27:4,9,14). It stresses the fact that Rebekah and Jacob were taking advantage of Isaac's appetite for a certain kind of food in order to trick him.

Another aspect of their trickery was to take advantage of Isaac's blindness by dressing Jacob in Esau's clothes and putting the goatskins on Jacob's hands and neck to make him smell and feel like Esau (27:15,16). Jacob, the deceiver *par excellence,* was tutored well by his equally deceitful mother!

Later, there would be divinely-ordained legislation prohibiting such deception of helpless people (Lev. 19:14; Deut. 27:18). But for now Rebekah simply brushed aside Jacob's fears and scoffed at the general revelation of God's will mediated to her through her conscience. And she did it with relish: "Your curse be on me, my son" (Gen. 27:13). We are reminded of the awful cry of the people of Jesus' day when Pontius Pilate offered to release Him: "His blood be on us and on our children!" (Matt. 27:25). Greedy people will sometimes even shake their fists in the face of God to get what they want.

Jacob followed his mother's instructions to the letter and then went into his father's room, pretending to be Esau (Gen. 27:19). Isaac was suspicious from the start, and his suspicions remained right to the end. He wondered how his son could have returned from the hunt so quickly (27:20); he wanted to touch his skin

(27:21); he thought he recognized Jacob's voice (27:22); he asked the young man a second time to identify himself (27:24). And throughout the entire charade, Jacob lied and lied and lied and lied!

If there is a single redeeming feature in this entire scene, it is perhaps this: Jacob was reluctant to call Isaac's God his own. He said, "The LORD *your* God caused it to happen to me" (27:20, italics added). Apparently Jacob didn't want to become personally involved with God's name while engaged in the act of deceiving his father.

But the crowning touch was the traitor's kiss (27:26,27). Jacob had become his father's Judas!

Finally, when Isaac smelled the clothes Jacob was wearing (they were *Esau's* clothes, of course), he gave him the blessing of the firstborn (27:27-29). He made Jacob the ruler of his brothers, present and future; he asked God to prosper him and he confirmed to him a section of God's call to and blessing on Abraham (see 12:3).

After the blessing, no sooner had Jacob gone out one door than Esau came in another, as it were. Esau too brought in a tasty meal and asked Isaac to bless him. In a clipped echo of his earlier question to Jacob (27:18), Isaac asked, "Who are *you?*" When Esau identified himself, Isaac trembled violently from head to toe because he realized that he had already blessed the wrong person. He then rhetorically asked who it was that he had blessed—blessed with a blessing that could not be revoked or retracted (27:33), because the spoken word in ancient times was believed to have the undeniable power of always accomplishing its purposes.

Both men knew who the deceiver had been, of course—but it was Esau who spoke his name: "Jacob"! Esau then commented on its meaning, "Supplanter," by stating that Jacob had supplanted him with respect to his blessing and his birthright. Esau continued to beg his father for at least one blessing, and then he broke down and wept bitterly (27:38).

It was too late for him to receive the main blessing, however (Heb. 12:17). The best he could hope for was a pitiful shadow or reflection of what Jacob had already received. And that's all Isaac could give him; compare the watered-down and essentially negative wording of Genesis 27:39 with the very similar but thoroughly positive wording of 27:28. A hint of the later hostility between the Edomites (descendants of Esau) and Israelites (descendants of Jacob) can be seen in 27:40. (See especially 2 Kings 8:20-22, an instance in which Edom did indeed "break the yoke" of Israel from their necks.)

Needless to say, Esau hated Jacob because of his deception and trickery, and he resolved to kill him after Isaac's death. When Rebekah heard about it, she told Jacob about Esau's plans. At the time of Sarah's death, Isaac had "comforted" himself by getting married (Gen. 24:67). Now, Esau hoped to "console" himself by killing his brother Jacob (27:42)! To Esau, murder was apparently just as valid a way to comfort oneself as marriage was!

Rebekah sternly warned Jacob that he should flee to Haran, where her brother Laban was living, until Esau had calmed down. She said to Jacob, "Obey my voice" (27:43)—a command that had gotten him into trouble before (27:8,13) but it was eminently sensible advice this time! She told Jacob to stay with Laban for "a few days" (27:44), which eventually lengthened into a period of 20 long years (31:38,41)!

But Rebekah's fears for Jacob's safety were entirely justified. She knew that Isaac's death would soon bring on Jacob's death at the hands of Esau, and she didn't want to have to mourn the loss of two members of her family at the same time (27:45).

A sordid story, this—full of greed, deceit, scheming, lying, jealousy, and murderous intent. Jacob's early life shows him to have been something less than a worthy grandson of Abraham. Because of a situation of his own making, he was forced to run away from home to escape his brother's anger.

Fortunately for Jacob, God had a better idea for his future— an idea that began to take shape in Genesis 28.

Footnote

1. See C. H. Gordon in D. N. Freedman and E. F. Campbell, Jr., editors, *The Biblical Archaeologist Reader, 2* (Garden City: Doubleday Anchor, 1964), pp. 23, 24.

8

JACOB:
His Years in Mesopotamia
Genesis 28:1—30:43

As we have already seen, the real reason for Jacob's trip to Haran was to escape Esau's anger (Gen. 27:43-45). But Rebekah, apparently not wanting to alarm Isaac, gave him the excuse that she didn't want Jacob to marry a Hittite girl (27:46) as Esau had done (26:34,35). How often we, too, conceal our real reasons for doing things by offering excuses in their place!

Jacob's Dream at Bethel—28:1-22

Excuse or not, Isaac shared Rebekah's fears concerning Jacob's future wife. So he sent Jacob off to *Paddan-aram* ("the plains of Aram"; see also 25:20), another name for northern Mesopotamia, where his grandfather Bethuel and his uncle Laban lived.

Using words similar to the ones Abraham had spoken to his

servant on a parallel occasion (24:3,4), Isaac told Jacob to marry one of Laban's daughters (28:2). He also prayed that God Almighty would give Jacob "the blessing of Abraham" (28:4; see 12:1-3), a blessing that we who are Gentile Christians have eventually come to share (see especially Gal. 3:14). Our share is spiritual, of course, while in Jacob's case the physical aspect of the blessing was dominant, emphasizing, as always, descendants and land.

When Esau heard that Jacob, with Isaac's benediction and blessing, had left for Mesopotamia to find a non-Canaanite wife, he decided to try to please his father by acting in a similar way. So, in addition to the Hittite wives he already had, he married an Ishmaelite girl (Gen. 28:9). That decision served only to stress the fact that Esau was not a spiritually discerning member of the covenant family.

Meanwhile Jacob had left Beersheba (28:10), where the family had been living (26:23), and he had departed for Haran. One evening he stopped for the night in a rock-strewn field and used one of the rocks as his pillow. To this very day, the area where Jacob slept presents a landscape characterized by outcroppings of rock with loose boulders and stones lying everywhere. In fact, he may have found it difficult to locate a rock-free place for his head even if he had wanted to! But however uncomfortable it may seem to us, Jacob used a rock for a pillow probably by choice rather than by necessity. In those days, headrests were often quite hard, sometimes even made of metal.[1]

After falling sound asleep, Jacob had a dream in which he saw a staircase (28:12; it was not a "ladder," which, in the modern sense at least, is a device with rungs). It was standing on the ground with its top reaching into the sky. The image in the dream was that of the sloping, stepped side of a particular type of Mesopotamian temple tower known technically as a *ziggurat*.

The Tower of Babel (11:1-9) was probably just such a ziggurat. In fact, the description of Jacob's staircase "with its top reaching to heaven" (28:12) parallels 11:4, where the builders were trying to erect a tower "whose top will reach into heaven." In fact, Mesopotamian ziggurats in ancient times bore such names as "House of the Link Between Heaven and Earth" or "House of the Seven Guides of Heaven and Earth." The Tower

82

of Babel itself was also known as "House of the Foundation-Platform of Heaven and Earth."[2]

But while the Tower of Babel came to symbolize confusion because of human arrogance (11:9), Jacob's staircase came to symbolize communion and fellowship with God, as we shall see (28:15). In Jacob's dream, the angels of God were ascending the staircase to bring Jacob's needs and prayers to the Lord and descending to bring the Lord's blessings and answers to Jacob.

The motif of the ascending and descending angels was referred to by Jesus in a memorable interview with Nathanael, one of His disciples. Jesus said to him, "You shall see the heavens opened, and the angels of God ascending and descending upon the Son of Man" (John 1:51). In making that beautiful statement, our Lord was picturing Himself as the true Bridge between heaven and earth. Jesus Christ is the real Ziggurat, the ultimate Staircase, the only genuine Mediator "between God and men" (1 Tim. 2:5). Jacob's dream of the staircase was fulfilled in Jesus.[3]

At the top of the ancient Mesopotamian ziggurat, the builders often set up a small shrine which they sometimes painted with blue enamel in order to make it blend in with the color of their god's celestial home. They believed that their deity would dwell in the shrine temporarily as he came down to meet with his people. The worshiper, then, would climb the outside staircase of the ziggurat all the way to the top, hoping to enjoy communion and fellowship with the god who would condescend to meet him in the little chapel.

Similarly, in Jacob's dream, at the top of the staircase stood God Himself (Gen. 28:13). He renewed the blessing of Abraham and Isaac to Jacob, again promising him the land of Canaan and numerous descendants. This time, the patriarchs' descendants were compared to the number of the specks of dust on the surface of the earth (28:14).

We can observe a beautiful progression in the figures of speech that God used to help the patriarchs visualize how many descendants they would have. They were to be as numerous as the stars in the sky (15:5), of which many thousands can be seen with the naked eye on a typical Near Eastern night. More than that, they were to be as numerous as the grains of sand along the seashore (22:17), a number difficult to comprehend, reaching certainly into billions upon billions and beyond. That might still turn out to be a theoretically manageable number, however, because (as someone might argue) the coastlines of the earth, however vast, are nevertheless limited.

But to have as many descendants as there are specks of dust on the earth (28:14)? Incredible! Who could possibly conceptualize that? A God who could afford to be so extravagant with His blessings must be infinitely great indeed! Dust, dust, dust— stretching in every direction as far as the eye could see or the mind conceive—what an image to help the ancient Israelite understand how our God fulfills His promises!

Pagan religions in those early days taught that gods were merely local deities who would protect their people only if those people stayed within the borders of their own tribal territories. But the God of the patriarchs assured Jacob, in effect, that He was not merely a tribal god. In fact, He promised to be with Jacob wherever he went, even if he left Canaan (28:15). Realizing that God never leaves His children has been a wonderful source of comfort and strength to believers down through the centuries (see again 26:3,24; 31:3; Matt. 28:20; Acts 18:10).

When Jacob awoke from his sleep, he realized that God must have been there even though he had been unaware of His presence at first. His frightened response was that this place then called Luz was awesome indeed, and he described it as "the house of God" and "the gate of heaven" (Gen. 28:17). Since *Babel* means literally "Gate of God" and since the Tower of Babel was also known as the "House of the Foundation-Platform of Heaven and Earth," Jacob's description serves to connect the staircase of his dream with the Mesopotamian ziggurats.

But his description also serves as a transition to renaming this town near which his dream occurred. He took the rock he had used as a headrest and set it up as a stone monument. Jacob's pillow now became a pillar. After pouring oil on top of it to consecrate it, he gave the name Bethel to the town that had been formerly known as Luz (28:19). The new name commemorated Jacob's experience there, since *"Bethel"* means "House of God" (28:17).

Finally, Jacob made a vow that had several conditions attached to it. He promised that if God would indeed be with him, and if He would protect him while he was traveling, and if He would supply him with the basic necessities of life, so that he would be able to return home safely (28:21; see also 33:18), then the Lord would be Jacob's God, the pillar would be God's house (in the sense that it would commemorate Jacob's meeting with God at Bethel). And last but not least Jacob would give to the Lord a tenth of everything he owned (28:22; see 14:20).

In summary, Jacob was promising God his life, his worship, and his possessions. Meeting God at Bethel was a critical stage in Jacob's relationship with Him.

We might even call it Jacob's conversion.

Jacob's Marriage—29:1-30

After his remarkable experience at Bethel, Jacob set out on foot for an area referred to by the word *qedem*, "east" (29:1). It was the region near Haran (29:4). A well was located there, and it had a large stone covering its mouth. In fact, so huge was the stone that the local shepherds were apparently reluctant to roll it away unless there happened to be enough thirsty sheep and goats nearby to make the effort worthwhile.

Jacob asked the shepherds who were there if they were acquainted with Laban, Nahor's "son" (29:5). (Laban was actually Nahor's grandson, but the Hebrew word "son" is a broad term that can refer, among other things, to any male descendant.) They told him they were, and then they pointed to Laban's daughter Rachel, a shepherdess, who was just arriving to give water to her father's sheep.

When Jacob saw her, he went over and singlehandedly rolled the stone from the well's mouth (29:10), clearly a feat of unusual strength. Then he kissed her and wept for joy—obviously a case of love at first sight!

Jacob told Rachel that he was related to her father through Rebekah. When she heard that, she ran and told Laban of Jacob's arrival, and then Laban in turn ran to greet him and bring him into his home.

After Laban had heard everything Jacob told him, he said to him, in essence, "You're really my own flesh and blood" (29:14).

His actual words, "Surely you are my bone and my flesh," were reminiscent of Adam's exclamation concerning Eve at the time of her creation (2:23): "This is now bone of my bones, and flesh of my flesh." (Blood kinship was not taken lightly in ancient times.) Once again, although the fact is not made explicit in the text, God had brought a descendant of Abraham to the right bride (see 24:48).

When Jacob had stayed with Laban for a month, Laban asked him to continue working for him for mutually agreeable wages. By now, Jacob had fallen deeply in love with Rachel, who was much more beautiful than her older sister Leah. So he told Laban that he would work seven years in exchange for the hand of Rachel in marriage.

Laban agreed immediately, and Jacob began to fulfill his unusual seven-year labor contract. Under such circumstances, we might guess that seven years would crawl along at a snail's pace. In this case, however, "they seemed to him but a few days because of his love for her" (29:20).

Unfortunately, Laban had secretly decided to give Jacob Leah instead of Rachel. Maybe he had tried unsuccessfully to marry her off earlier, and now he saw his chance.

His plan was deceptively simple. At the end of the seven years, Laban prepared the customary wedding feast honoring the new bride. Then, after dark, he sent Leah into Jacob's tent. It was not until morning that Jacob realized he had been tricked. And by that time it was too late to do anything about it, because he had already cohabited with Leah.

How could Laban's scheme have turned out so successfully? Wasn't Jacob able to distinguish between the two girls because of the darkness? Did Leah's veil (see 24:65) conceal her identity? Had Jacob become intoxicated by the wine served at the wedding feast? Or was it a combination of these three factors?

Whatever the reason, Jacob had obviously met his match in Laban. The deceiver had been deceived! Jacob had deceived Esau, and now Laban had deceived Jacob. "Whatever a man sows, this he will also reap" (Gal. 6:7).

Jacob, understandably, was upset and thoroughly disgusted. He had worked hard for seven years and still hadn't won the hand of Rachel, so he asked Laban for an explanation. Laban pleaded local custom as his excuse. "It is not the practice in our place," he said, "to marry off the younger before the firstborn" (Gen. 29:26). Then Laban generously agreed to give Rachel to Jacob in exchange for *another* seven years of work!

Having no recourse under the law, at least to his knowledge, Jacob consented. The seven days of Leah's wedding feast were concluded as originally intended (29:28; see also Judg. 14:17). Jacob then received Rachel as his second wife, and seven more years of work began.

Taking everything into consideration, it is no wonder that Jacob "loved Rachel more than Leah" (Gen. 29:30)!

Fertility in Family and Flock—29:31—30:43

Because Leah was less loved than Rachel, the Lord took pity on her and gave her a son, Jacob's firstborn. Genesis 29:31—30:24 tells the story of the birth of 11 of Jacob's sons. The Hebrew love of punning is evident in the individual accounts of why each son was given a particular name.

1. *Reuben* was Jacob's firstborn son. His name means "See, a son!" and is related to Leah's observation that God had "seen" her affliction (29:32). Similarly, *Ishmael*, which means "God hears," had been so named because God had "heard" Hagar's cry of affliction (16:11).

2. Likewise *Simeon* ("hearing"), Jacob's second son, was given his name because the Lord had "heard" that Leah was unloved (29:33) by her husband.

3. *Levi* was born next. His name means "attachment" and reflects Leah's desire that now her husband would become "attached" to her because she had borne him three sons (29:34).

It is noteworthy that these first three boys were given names that mirror Leah's unhappy relationship with Jacob, a situation that was not of her own making.

4. *Judah* ("praise") was so named because when he was born Leah said, "I will praise the LORD" (29:35). In this case no comment is made about Leah's relationship to Jacob, perhaps in anticipation of the fact that in later years Judah gained in prominence and eventually became the most important of Jacob's 12 sons.

Meanwhile, Rachel began to envy Leah's fertility. She wanted very much to have children of her own (30:1; see also 30:24) and said to Jacob, "Give me children, or else I die." (Her words were ironically and tragically prophetic, because she died in labor when Jacob's twelfth son, Benjamin, was born; see 35:18.)

But Jacob, of course, replied, "Am I in the place of God?" Joseph would respond similarly in a different situation years later (50:19). Both men were reminding the people to whom they were speaking that God is sovereign, that He does as He pleases, and that we cannot overrule His purposes.[4]

Rachel sheepishly realized that she had blamed Jacob for something that wasn't his fault. So she then told him to cohabit with her servant girl, Bilhah, and produce a son through her (30:3). Jacob's grandmother, Sarah, had made a similar suggestion to Abraham many years before (16:2). As we pointed out earlier (see chap. 3), the legal sanction behind such proposals has been amply illustrated by contract documents found at Nuzi. But the morality of Rachel's demand is no less questionable than that of Sarah had been, of course.

Bilhah, said Rachel, was to bear the child "on my knees" (30:3), a phrase symbolic of adoption procedure and indicating that Rachel intended to adopt the newborn child as her own.

Jacob consented to Rachel's request, and Bilhah became his concubine (35:22) for the purpose of bearing children.

5. So *Dan* was born to Jacob and Rachel through Bilhah. His name means "He argued the case," since God had, in effect, argued Rachel's case by hearing her plea and vindicating her cause (30:6).

6. The sixth son, *Naphtali* ("my wrestling"), was also born to Bilhah. He was so named because Rachel had "wrestled" with her sister Leah (figuratively, of course!) and had won the battle (30:8).

7. As Rachel had given her servant girl Bilhah to Jacob as a concubine, so Leah now gave her servant girl, Zilpah, to him. Through Zilpah the seventh son, *Gad*, was born. His name, meaning "fortune," reflects Leah's joyful cry at his birth: "How fortunate!" (30:11).

8. *Asher* ("happy") was also born to Zilpah. He was given that name because at his birth Leah exclaimed, "Happy am I! For women will call me happy" (30:13).

Jacob's firstborn son Reuben, by now old enough to play in the fields, found some mandrake plants there one day and brought them to his mother Leah. "The peculiar shape of the large, fleshy, forked roots, which resemble the lower part of the human body, gave rise to a popular superstition that the mandrake would induce conception."[5] Rachel, who at this stage of her life probably believed that superstition, asked Leah for some of Reuben's mandrakes.

Leah agreed, but only if Rachel would allow Jacob to cohabit with Leah that night. (Apparently Rachel, as Jacob's favorite wife, had the questionable privilege of deciding which of Jacob's wives or concubines he would sleep with on any given night.) Out of this arrangement, tainted by superstition and sordidness, came the next son. God certainly works in mysterious ways sometimes!

9. *Issachar,* Leah's fifth son, was Jacob's ninth. His name means "he is hired" because, as Leah said, "God has given me my wages, because I gave my maid to my husband" (30:18). She had also told Jacob earlier that she had "hired" him in exchange for Reuben's mandrakes (30:16).

10. Leah's sixth son was Jacob's tenth. Leah was sure that Jacob would now "honor" her because she had borne him six sons, so she named the newborn baby *Zebulun* ("honored," 30:20).

11. Jacob's eleventh child was actually a daughter named Dinah, but since daughters were considered less important than sons in those days, nothing more is said of her here (30:21). Instead we are told that God now "remembered" Rachel in her distress, just as He had remembered Noah in his (8:1) and would later remember Hannah in hers (1 Sam. 1:19,20). To "remember" in such situations did not mean to recall something that had been temporarily forgotten. It meant, rather, to "pay special attention to" or "lovingly care for" someone. So God remembered Rachel, paid attention to her needs, and gave her a son of her own. The newborn baby was named *Joseph,* meaning "may He add," because of Rachel's plea that God would add to her yet another son (30:24).

The fulfillment of that plea would result in Rachel's death (35:16-18). But, in the meantime, Jacob had become the father of

89

eleven sons and one daughter through four different wives. His family had become fertile indeed, and God was obviously blessing them lavishly.

God's blessings of fertility on Jacob's family were matched by His blessings of fertility on Jacob's flocks, a subject that occupies the remainder of Genesis 30. Now that Rachel had given birth to a son, Jacob felt that it was about time for him to begin the trip back to Canaan. So he asked Laban to allow him to leave with his wives and children.

The crafty Laban, however, could see that he had a good thing going for him. He had observed that God was blessing Jacob (30:27). Similar observations had been made by other men concerning Abraham (21:22) and Isaac (26:28) in former years. Jacob's prosperity is an illustration of the fact that when a man of God's choice is doing a good job, his employer will usually want to keep him around for as long as possible.

So Laban asked Jacob to name his wages and stay in Mesopotamia. Jacob finally agreed, requesting as his wages only the spotted and mottled animals in Laban's flocks. Laban readily consented to Jacob's request, but then he secretly removed all such animals from his flocks without telling Jacob he was doing so.

Nevertheless, Jacob had apparently already formulated his own plans for breeding animals with spotted or mottled coloration. He went and gathered some "poplar" and other twigs and cut "white" streaks in them, exposing some of the "white" wood of the twigs (30:37). The Hebrew words for "poplar" and "white" are puns on the name "Laban," which means "white." Jacob's scheme was saying in effect, "I'll give Laban some of his own medicine!"

Jacob placed the twigs in conspicuous positions near the watering troughs that Laban's animals were accustomed to using. The animals would see the twigs when they came to drink, and Jacob superstitiously hoped that they would then produce mottled young because they had seen mottled wood!

Amazingly enough, things turned out exactly as he had planned. But we can be sure that it was God's power and not Jacob's superstition that brought about the desired results.

During the next six years (31:41), Jacob became very wealthy

(30:43). Whatever faith he may have had in his own superstitious practices, it is to his credit that he was willing to admit that ultimately it was God who had made him prosperous (31:9).

Footnotes

1. See, for example, Plate 8 in C. Aldred, *The Egyptians* (New York: Frederick A. Praeger, Inc., 1961); Plate 90 in P. Montet, *Eternal Egypt* (New York: New American Library of World Literature, Inc., 1964).

2. See A. Parrot, *The Tower of Babel* (New York: Philosophical Library, 1955).

3. R. Youngblood, *Special Day Sermons* (Grand Rapids: Baker Book House, 1973), pp. 31-40.

4. See R. Youngblood, *The Heart of the Old Testament* (Grand Rapids: Baker Book House, 1971), pp. 17-26.

5. *Fauna and Flora of the Bible* (London: United Bible Societies, 1972), p. 139.

9

JACOB:

His Return Home
Genesis 31:1–36:43

By this time, Jacob had been living in Mesopotamia for 20 years (Gen. 31:38,41). He had married two wives, acquired two concubines and become the father of eleven sons and one daughter. He had also accumulated a great amount of wealth.

Surely, the time was now ripe for him to go back to Canaan.

Jacob's Departure from Laban—31:1-55
Several factors made Jacob decide to return home. For one thing, Laban's sons were complaining that Jacob had become wealthy at their father's expense (31:1). This meant, of course, that their own inheritance had been severely reduced. So it was likely that they would become angry with Jacob, and their anger could easily erupt into violence.

Also, Laban himself had begun to look at Jacob with disfavor. Jacob could tell that things were not the same between them as they had been before in happier days (31:2,5).

In addition to this, Rachel and Leah felt that their father Laban had cheated them out of their own share of the family inheritance by stupidly allowing Jacob to take it over bit by bit. They came to the conclusion that their future security lay elsewhere, with Jacob, and so they encouraged him to leave Laban and take them along with him (31:14-16).

But finally, and overriding every other consideration, was the fact that it was God's will for Jacob to leave Mesopotamia and return to Canaan. Circumstances sometimes may seem to compel us to undertake a certain course of action. But before we act, we should be as sure as we can that God is in it.

In Jacob's case the Lord specifically told him that he was to go back to Canaan (31:3,13). As before, so also now, God promised to accompany Jacob with His protecting presence (31:3; see also 31:5). Jacob told his wives that Laban had cheated him by changing his wages ten times (31:7; see also 31:41), but that in spite of Laban's deceit God had stepped in and made Jacob prosperous (31:7-9). (Even Jacob's own superstitious attempts to increase the size of his flocks as recorded in 30:31-43 were successful only because God overruled, as Jacob himself finally seemed to realize; see 31:9.) Clinching his decision to return to Canaan was a dream in which Jacob heard the angel of the Lord, speaking in the name of the God of Bethel, command him to go back home (31:11-13).

So every signal Jacob was receiving—from Laban, from Laban's sons, from Jacob's own wives, from God Himself— indicated to him that all systems were "go" and that he should prepare to leave as soon as possible (31:17,18).

But two clouds hung over the scene of Jacob's potential departure.

First, Jacob had deceived Laban by not telling him that he was leaving (31:20). Jacob had already crossed the Euphrates (the "river" of 31:21; see also 15:18) and was headed for Gilead, a territory northeast of the Sea of Galilee, before Laban found out he had left. Laban took some men with him and set out in pursuit. But one night during the chase God warned Laban not to harm Jacob (31:24).

When he finally overtook Jacob, Laban scolded him for deceiving him. He told Jacob that had he known he was leaving he would have given him and his family a royal farewell. "Why did you flee secretly?" he asked (31:27). Jacob's only response was that he was afraid Laban would have taken his daughters away from him by force (31:31).

Secondly, and to complicate matters even further, Rachel had stolen Laban's *teraphim* (household idols) while Laban had been away from home shearing sheep (31:19). Why she had done so is debatable. Many scholars have felt that possession of a man's household idols was tantamount to possessing the rights to his estate after his death. Contract tablets from Nuzi have been used to support this idea.[1]

It seems, however, that intentional bequeathal and not mere possession of such idols was necessary to give the holder the right to take over the original owner's inheritance. It is possible, then, that Rachel took the idols simply because she was going on a journey and wanted to have objects of worship along with her. We know that similar practices occurred in the Near East hundreds of years later, as Josephus tells us.[2] Rachel, after all, was probably not yet completely free of her polytheistic background and beliefs (see Josh. 24:2 and especially Gen. 35:2).

At any rate, Laban became angry when he found out his "gods" (31:30) had been stolen. He asked Jacob why he had taken them, apparently feeling that Jacob was the most likely thief. Laban had come to know Jacob fairly well by this time!

But Jacob didn't know that Rachel had taken the idols. So he told Laban that if he could find them among the belongings of anyone in Jacob's party, that person would be put to death (31:32). Such a vow, even made in all innocence, can be very dangerous, as Joseph's brothers were to discover years later (44:6-12)!

Jacob told Laban to go ahead and look around if he wanted to. Laban did so, but he couldn't find the idols because Rachel had hidden them in her camel saddle and was sitting on them. She apologized to her father for not getting up to pay him the respect due to him, but stated that she couldn't get up because she was having her monthly period (31:35).

In later generations the Law of Moses would stipulate that a woman in that condition was ritually unclean (Lev. 15:19) and that may have been true even here.

We must not miss the humor of this scene and its contrast with the majesty and power of the one true God. False gods like Laban's are so small and so helpless that they can be hidden in a camel saddle and sat on by a menstruating woman!

And now it was Jacob's turn to become angry. He scolded Laban for what he thought was a false accusation. He then pointed out to him that Laban had gotten the better of the deal in every way during the 20 years of their business relationship (Gen. 31:36-41). He ended his tirade by saying, "If the God of my father, the God of Abraham, and the fear of Isaac, had not been for me, surely now you would have sent me away empty-handed" (31:42).

Jacob had referred to God as "the God of my father" also in 31:5, and Laban, speaking to Jacob, had called Him "the God of your father" in 31:29. Here, in 31:42, Jacob identified Him more specifically as "the God of Abraham, and the fear of Isaac" (see also 31:53).

If the word "fear" is correctly translated here and is intended as a title for God, we should probably understand it in the sense of "Revered One." But it has also been suggested that it means "kinsman."[3] If the former is the right translation, the title refers to God's holiness, His aloofness, His transcendence. But if the word means "kinsman," the reference would be to God's closeness, His nearness, His immanence. Although we cannot be absolutely certain of the correct translation, the latter would fit in well with the intimate relationship the patriarchs enjoyed with their God.

Laban didn't back down from his claims of ownership over his daughters, grandchildren and flocks. But he did recognize, of course, that his daughters had every right to accompany their husband Jacob back to Canaan, if they wished to do so (31:43). So Laban proposed that he and Jacob make a covenant between them, a covenant to be solemnized by offering a sacrifice (31:54; see also 15:9-11,17,18; Exod. 24:5-8) and sharing a meal (Gen. 31:46; see also Exod. 24:11). The covenant they entered into was a kind of nonaggression pact in which Laban and Jacob promised not to deceive each other or trespass on one another's territory (31:50,52).

To mark the boundary between them, Jacob set up a rock as a pillar (31:45-48). He also had his men gather stones and pile them up into a mound. Each man gave the mound a name in his own language; Laban the Aramean (see 31:24) called it *Jegar-sahadutha* (Aramaic for "mound of witness"), while Jacob the Hebrew called it *Galeed* (Hebrew for "mound of witness"; for the later naming of an altar in a similar way, see Josh. 22:34).

It was also called *Mizpah* ("watchtower") because Laban said to Jacob, "May the LORD watch between you and me when we are absent one from the other" (Gen. 31:49). This statement is sometimes called the "Mizpah benediction" and is well known and beloved among many Christian groups. Unfortunately, however, Laban and Jacob were in no mood to wish each other well or to ask God to protect them while they were separated from each other. The context indicates that Laban's statement should be understood to mean something like this: "May the LORD keep an eye on you and me while we're separated from each other"— to keep each man from cheating or deceiving the other! So the "Mizpah benediction" turns out to be a malediction, or at best a negative benediction!

The mound and pillar were set up as boundary markers between the northern territory where Laban lived and the territory to the south where Jacob would once again live (31:52). They were set up in the hill country of Gilead (31:25,54). (Jacob's name for the mound, *Galeed,* is a pun on "Gilead.")

Each man took a solemn oath to abide by the terms of the covenant.

On the one hand, Laban's oath seems to intentionally reflect his polytheism, his belief in many so-called "gods." The verb in 31:53 is plural, and his oath can be translated, "The god(s) of Abraham and the god(s) of Nahor, the god(s) of their father, judge between us." In other words, Laban took his oath in the name of Terah's god or gods (see Josh. 24:2).

Jacob, on the other hand, took his oath in the name of the one true God, the God of his father Isaac (31:53), the God whom Jacob had met and worshiped at Bethel 20 years earlier (28:13).

The two men had now finally made their decision to separate from each other, so the next morning Laban kissed his daughters and grandchildren goodbye and then went home (31:55). ("Bless" often means simply "say goodbye"; see especially 47:7,10.)

Jacob's Meeting with Esau—32:1—33:20

Before he could return confidently and safely (33:18) to Canaan, Jacob would have to settle accounts with his brother Esau, whom he had cheated out of his birthright and blessing (27:36). When Jacob had left Canaan, his life had been tainted with treachery and deceit. But since then he had had a profound spiritual experience, so his relationship with Esau would have to be made right. Our fellowship with God can never be complete until we become reconciled with people we have wronged. In Jacob's case, even before meeting Esau again he would meet God again, as we shall see.

After leaving Laban, Jacob continued on his way accompanied by the angels of God (32:1). Their presence no doubt reminded Jacob that God had promised to be with him always (28:15; see also 28:12; 31:11,13).

When he saw the angels, Jacob exclaimed, "This is God's camp" (32:2). In commemoration of his vision, the place where Jacob saw them was named *Mahanaim,* which means "two camps" or "two armies." Its location is uncertain, but it was situated somewhere in Gilead east of the Jordan river and north of the Jabbok river. The name anticipated also the "two companies" into which Jacob would soon divide his household and herds (32:7,10).

The presence of the angels must have comforted and reassured Jacob, at least to some extent. As a psalmist of a later generation said, "The angel of the LORD encamps around those who fear Him, and rescues them" (Ps. 34:7).

But Jacob realized that Esau might very well still be angry with him, so he decided to take the necessary precautions. He sent messengers on ahead of him to Esau (Gen. 32:3). When they arrived, they were to refer to Esau as Jacob's "lord" and to Jacob as Esau's "servant" (32:4,5; see also 32:18,20) in order to stress Jacob's humility.

When the messengers returned, they told Jacob that Esau was coming to meet him with an army of 400 men. Greatly frightened by this news, Jacob divided his household and animals into two groups, so that if Esau attacked one group the other would have a chance to escape (32:6-8).

He also sent a large number of animals to Esau as a gift. He

97

divided them into three separate herds to be presented to Esau at intervals, hoping to calm him down gradually before Jacob himself arrived (32:13-21).

But before he sent the animals, Jacob prayed to God for mercy, reminding Him that He had advised him to go back to Canaan (32:9; see 31:13) and that He had promised to give him a large number of descendants (32:12; see 28:14). Jacob was acting on the important truth that when a believer gets into a difficult situation, he should go to God in prayer immediately and not do so only as a last resort.

That same night, Jacob sent the members of his immediate family across the Jabbok river (today called the Wadi Zerqa, a stream flowing westward into the Jordan river about 20 miles north of the Dead Sea). Left alone, Jacob suddenly found himself wrestling with "a man" (32:24) in a struggle that lasted till daybreak. Hosea 12:3,4 identifies Jacob's opponent as God Himself in the person of an angel.

This strange wrestling match ended in a draw with no absolutely clear victor. But the angel managed to dislocate Jacob's hip (32:25), causing him to walk with a limp after that time (32:31) and resulting in a later Israelite dietary prohibition (32:32).

But Jacob refused to let the angel go until the angel agreed to bless him (32:26,29). The angel changed Jacob's name from *Jacob* ("supplanter") to *Israel* ("God fights" or "he fights with God"), because he had fought with God and emerged victorious, at least to some extent (32:28). God would later confirm Jacob's change of name (35:10), and the fact that Jacob had become Israel would often be recalled in later generations (1 Kings 18:31; 2 Kings 17:34). Jacob's little family would eventually grow and become the mighty nation of Israel.

Jacob, in turn, asked the angel what *his* name was, but he refused to tell him (Gen. 32:29). He indicated that there was no need for Jacob to know that fact (see the similar refusal expressed by the angel of the Lord in another situation recorded in Judg. 13:17,18).

To commemorate the wrestling match and its consequences, Jacob named the place where it happened *Peniel* (Gen. 32:30), elsewhere always spelled Penuel (see, for example, 32:31; both words mean "the face of God"). The exact location of the site is unknown, but it could not have been too far from the Jabbok river. Like Hagar before him, Jacob thought he had seen God face to face and was therefore surprised that he was still alive (32:30; see 16:13). Similar situations are recorded also in Judges 6:22; 13:22.

Jacob's experience at Penuel is a fine example of persistence in faith and prayer.[4] Fearless in his struggle with God, he now had nothing to fear in his meeting with Esau. Genesis 33 displays Jacob's courtesy toward his brother but is completely silent about the fear he had shown earlier. Similarly, our lives will be spiritually vital only as we strengthen them with persistent prayer.

When Jacob saw Esau coming with his 400 men, he divided his wives and children into three groups in the order of their importance in his eyes. He then lined the groups up, one behind the other, keeping the most important group (Rachel and Joseph) in the rear (Gen. 33:1,2). He himself led the way, bowing down to the ground seven times as he approached Esau (33:3). This was a sign of total and abject humility, as certain fourteenth-century-B.C. documents found at Tell el-Amarna in Egypt demonstrate.[5]

But Esau ran forward to meet him, and the two brothers enjoyed a tearful reunion (33:4). As he had instructed his messengers to do (32:3-5,17-20), Jacob also referred to himself as Esau's "servant" and to Esau as his "lord" (33:5,8,13-15). But Esau generously insisted on calling Jacob his "brother" (33:9), obviously willing to let bygones be bygones.

After Jacob had introduced his family to Esau (33:5-7; with 33:5 compare 48:8,9), he insisted that Esau accept the gift of animals he had offered him. Then, not wanting to go to Seir, Esau's homeland, Jacob told Esau to go on ahead. He gave him the excuse that his children and animals were weak and that he didn't want to delay Esau (33:12-16).

When Esau had left, Jacob went on to a place called *Succoth*, which means "shelters." There he built a house for himself and shelters for his animals. We cannot say for certain where Succoth was located, but it was east of the Jordan river and on a more or less direct line between Penuel (32:31) and Shechem (33:18).

At long last, Jacob crossed the Jordan and arrived at Shechem in central Canaan. The Lord had answered Jacob's prayer of 20 years earlier that he might return to his homeland "safely" (33:18; see 28:21). The "few days" that Rebekah had expected Jacob to spend in Mesopotamia (27:44) had stretched into many long years. But God, in His own good time, had now brought Jacob home. Our prayers are *always* answered, even if not always in the way we expect them to be.

The plot of ground where Jacob pitched his tent near Shechem he purchased for 100 "pieces of money" from the sons of Hamor the Hivite. Since *Hamor* means "donkey," it is possible that Hamor and Sons were donkey caravanners, as the patriarchs themselves may have been (see chap. 1). The Hebrew word translated "piece of money" is *qesitah,* found only twice elsewhere and always in patriarchal contexts (Josh. 24:32; Job 42:11).

Jacob or his men dug a well near Shechem. Mentioned in John 4:5,6, "Jacob's well" can still be visited at the present time. It is one of the few clearly authentic ancient sites to be seen in the Holy Land today. The well is deep, and its water is cold and delicious.

At Shechem, Jacob built an altar and named it *El-Elohe-Israel* ("God, the God of Israel") in gratitude to God for bringing him safely home. In so doing, Jacob was following a practice begun by his grandfather Abraham, who had a habit of building altars at places where he had significant spiritual experiences (Gen. 12:7; 13:18; 22:9).

Jacob's response to God was the correct one. God had answered his prayer, and so Jacob, with heartfelt thanks, worshiped Him (33:20).

Are we as ready to thank God for answered prayer as Jacob was?

The Rape of Dinah—34:1-31

The title of this section could just as easily be "the rape of the city of Shechem."

Genesis 34 is one of the most sordid chapters in the entire Bible. It tells a story of rape, anger, deceit, greed, murder, violence, and selfishness. God's name appears twice in the place-name that ends Genesis 33, and God's name begins Genesis 35; but it is no wonder that the name of God doesn't appear even once in all of Genesis 34!

The city of Shechem had its namesake in one of the sons of Hamor the Hivite (33:19; 34:2). The young Shechem was the most honored, and perhaps pampered, member of his family (34:19). He was no doubt accustomed to getting just about anything he wanted. So when he saw and desired Jacob's daughter Dinah, he seized her and raped her.

It often happens that after a man has committed the sin of rape, his desire turns to disgust. This is what took place, for example, after David's son Amnon had raped his half-sister, Tamar (2 Sam. 13:10-15).

The reverse was true in the case of Shechem, however. After he had raped Dinah, he fell in love with her (Gen. 34:3). In both instances, of course, the act of rape was disgraceful and vile (34:7; 2 Sam. 13:12). And in Dinah's case, her brothers were enraged when they heard about it.

But Shechem had meanwhile told his father Hamor that he wanted to marry Dinah (Gen. 34:4). Hamor was pleased with the idea, so he told Dinah's father and brothers that intermarriage between their two families would be mutually beneficial. As for Shechem, he offered to bring as large a "bridal payment and gift" as Jacob and his sons wanted (34:12). But what Jacob's sons really wanted was revenge!

So they deceitfully agreed to the marriage of Shechem and Dinah, but only on the condition that all the males in the city of Shechem agree to be circumcised, just as all the males in Jacob's family had been (34:15). Jacob's sons had obviously learned a few dirty tricks from their father's previous example in his own moments of sinful weakness. And now they were about to use the holy ceremony of circumcision—the sign of the Abrahamic covenant—as a tool to further their wicked plans! No sin is more despicable than to press the sacred into service for profane uses.

Hamor and Shechem were completely duped by the suggestion of Jacob's sons. So they made a formal proposal to all the male Shechemites at the gateway of the city, the normal forum for legal activity and discussion in ancient times (34:20; see also 23:10; Ruth 4:11). We note that the ulterior motive of greed entered into their decision, since they felt that they would gain in wealth at the expense of the Israelites (Gen. 34:23). And so the fateful circumcision took place.

Men weakened by pain and loss of blood are no match for healthy, angry men. Simeon and Levi, two of Jacob's sons, counted on that fact. And they were fiendishly correct: they were easily able to kill all the male Shechemites and retrieve Dinah from Shechem's house. The sons of Jacob then came and plundered the city of all its wealth, taking its women and children captive as well.

The vengeance they meted out was terrible indeed. Even though a woman had been raped—and that was the only excuse Simeon and Levi had (34:31)—the punishment far exceeded the crime. At any rate, two wrongs never make a right—nor does might make right.

And all Jacob could think of was his own reputation! Never mind the fact that his daughter had been raped, or that every male citizen of Shechem had been slaughtered, or that the city itself had been plundered, or that its women and children had been taken captive, or that Jacob's sons had degraded and dehumanized themselves by committing acts of unspeakable wickedness. Jacob's ego had now been hurt, and he thought only of his lowered standing among the local inhabitants. His selfish response to the violence and bloodshed his sons had perpetrated is highlighted by his use of "me," "my" and "I" no less than eight times in 34:30!

As for Simeon and Levi, Jacob's deathbed blessing would turn out to be a curse for them (49:5-7). Their descendants would be scattered far and wide because of the terrible crime at Shechem.

A sordid chapter indeed! Genesis 34 remains a solemn example of how deep in sin it is possible for people to sink!

Jacob's Return to Bethel—35:1-29

We are not told how much time elapsed between the events of Genesis 34 and those of Genesis 35. But, sooner or later, God told Jacob to leave Shechem and go southward to Bethel. There he was to build an altar to the Lord, who had appeared to him at Bethel more than 20 years before (35:1; 28:13).

Jacob wanted to make sure that the members of his household

were not ritually unclean when they made the trip. So he told them, among other things, to get rid of their foreign "gods." the idols that Rachel and perhaps others had brought along with them (35:2; 31:19,30,34). After gathering the idols together, Jacob buried them under a large tree near Shechem (35:4).

As always, God was with Jacob (35:3) just as He had promised He would be (28:15); and the fear of Him protected Jacob and his household as they traveled (35:5). When he arrived at Bethel, he built the altar that God had commanded him to build and he named it *El-bethel* ("the God of Bethel").

At about the same time Deborah, Rebekah's nurse who had accompanied her all the way from Mesopotamia (24:59) and may even have outlived her (the last reference to Rebekah alive is 29:12), died and was buried under an oak tree near Bethel. The mourning and weeping that took place at her death gave rise to the name *Allon-bacuth* ("oak of weeping") for that spot (35:8).

God "again" appeared to Jacob and confirmed to him his new name, Israel (35:9,10; see 32:28). As He had revealed Himself to Abraham as "God Almighty" when telling him that he would be the ancestor of numerous descendants who would occupy the land of Canaan (17:1-8), so now He did also to Jacob (35:11,12). By himself, Jacob could not possibly succeed in producing descendants or conquering the land, of course. But with God Almighty on his side, Jacob could not possibly fail in doing so.

In gratitude for God's continued promise of help, Jacob again set up a pillar and consecrated it at the very place he had earlier named *Bethel* ("house of God," 35:14,15; see 28:18,19). In so doing, he renewed his vows of commitment to the Lord.

Jacob and his household then left Bethel and continued southward. Rachel was in the last stages of pregnancy, and she began to have severe labor pains while the group was traveling. The midwife assisting her told her not to be afraid, assuring her that she was going to have another son (35:17). Her words to Rachel were strangely reminiscent of Rachel's own plea when Joseph had been born (30:24). Sadly enough, she died in childbirth (35:18) in ironic and tragic fulfillment of another earlier plea she had made (30:1).

Just before Rachel died, she named Jacob's newborn son *Ben-oni* ("son of my misfortune"). Jacob, however, soon renamed the boy *Benjamin,* which means "son of the right hand" or "son of the south." These two possible translations of the name are related, since one set of ancient Hebrew terms for indications of direction was based on facing toward the east, in which case south was the direction to the right. Benjamin was the ancestor of one of the Israelite tribes that eventually settled in southern Canaan. During the patriarchal period itself, a Semitic tribe with a name very similar to that of Benjamin was located in a region situated to the south of certain other tribes, according to the Mari letters.[6]

Rachel was the only one of the wives of the three patriarchs— Abraham, Isaac and Jacob—who was not buried in the cave of Machpelah at Hebron alongside her husband (see 49:29-32). Instead, she was buried beside the road leading to Ephrath (the older name for Bethlehem; see the great Messianic prophecy in Micah 5:2, where the two names are combined as "Bethlehem Ephrathah"; see also Ruth 1:2).

Jacob marked Rachel's grave with a tombstone (Gen. 35:20), and its location was still known in Samuel's time (1 Sam. 10:2). Even today a site near Bethlehem called "Rachel's tomb" is pointed out by guides and visited by tourists, although in this case we can't be sure of its authenticity.

Jacob settled down in that general area for a time. While the family was there, Reuben cohabited with his father's concubine, Bilhah, on at least one occasion (35:22). Although he was Jacob's firstborn (35:23), he lost his pre-eminent position because of his sin (49:3,4; 1 Chron. 5:1).

The birth of Benjamin, Jacob's twelfth son, now made the roster of Jacob's sons complete, so they were conveniently listed in the record at this point (Gen. 35:22-26). Then, still continuing southward, Jacob finally arrived at his father's home in Mamre or Kiriath-arba (older names for Hebron). Isaac died at the age of 180 and was buried by his sons Esau and Jacob (35:28,29).

Abraham and Isaac were now off the scene. Although Jacob still had 27 years of life ahead of him, he was already 120 years old at the time of Isaac's death (see 25:26; 47:28). The old order was rapidly disappearing, and the focus of attention was about to shift from the older patriarchs to the younger ones and from Canaan to Egypt.

The Generations of Esau—36:1-43

Helping us to catch our breath as we move from the old order to the new is Genesis 36, another section of "connective tissue." An earlier example had to do with Ishmael's descendants (25:12-18), while this one is concerned with the descendants of Esau.

Genesis 36 begins and ends with the information that Esau was the ancestor of the Edomites. *Edom* means "Red" (see also 25:30), and the territory of the Edomites was located southeast and south of the Dead Sea where reddish-hued rock formations are a conspicuous feature of the landscape.

The names of Esau's wives in 36:2,3 differ somewhat from those in 26:34 and 28:9. Some say these discrepancies are errors that crept into the text as it was copied and recopied from generation to generation. It is equally possible, however, that Esau's wives had alternate names (Esau himself, after all, was also known as Edom), or even that Esau had more than three wives.

The land of Edom was also called *Seir* (36:8; see also 32:3), a name related to the Hebrew word for "hair." We are reminded that *Esau* also means "hairy" (see 25:25). Esau apparently drove out the original Horite (Hurrian) inhabitants of Seir (14:6), whose family tree is recorded in 36:20-30.

A total of 12 Edomite tribes is listed in 36:11-14 (5 in 36:11, 4 in 36:13, and 3 in 36:14). The frequently recurring pattern of 12 tribes is believed by some scholars to be related to the supposed practice of each tribe supplying the needs of their central sanctuary for one month of the year.[7] We have already observed the pattern in the case of the descendants of Nahor (22:20-24), Ishmael (25:13-16), and Jacob himself (35:22-26). Incidentally, we should also note that "son" in Genesis 36 could in some cases mean "grandson" or, more broadly, "descendant," in accord with general Hebrew usage elsewhere in the Old Testament.

As Genesis 14:14 apparently contains a later editorial touch in its mention of Dan (long before the town in question was called by that name), so also Genesis 36:31 seems to imply a later editorial touch in the way in which it mentions Israelite kings (long before the time of the Israelite monarchy).[8] But since other Old Testament books, like the Psalms, were compiled over a period of centuries, such editorial updating to help later readers shouldn't alarm or even surprise us.

Our doctrine of inspiration isn't affected one bit by such observations. The same God who inspired the original author (or authors, in the case of a book like Proverbs) of an Old Testament book also inspired its compilers and editors, if any. The final product, the completed Word of God, is just as inspired and infallible and authoritative as each individual word and verse and chapter and book that entered into its compilation. And we should be grateful for whatever God's people in ancient times, "moved by the Holy Spirit" (2 Pet. 1:21), did to clarify that Word for us.

Footnotes

1. See, for example, E. A. Speiser in G. A. Buttrick, editor, *The Interpreter's Dictionary of the Bible, K-Q* (Nashville: Abingdon Press, 1962), pp. 573, 574.

2. Josephus, *Antiquities* (XVIII, 9, 5).

3. W. F. Albright, *From the Stone Age to Christianity,* second edition (Baltimore: The Johns Hopkins Press, 1957), p. 248.

4. G. Vos, *Biblical Theology* (Grand Rapids: Wm. B. Eerdmans Publishing Company, 1948), pp. 111-114.

5. See, for example, W. F. Albright in J. B. Pritchard, editor, *Ancient Near Eastern Texts,* second edition; (Princeton: Princeton University Press), pp. 483-490.

6. See W. F. Albright, *Yahweh and the Gods of Canaan* (Garden City: Doubleday & Company, Inc., 1968), pp. 78, 79.

7. See M. Noth, *The History of Israel,* revised edition (New York: Harper and Brothers, 1960), pp. 85-91.

8. See, for example, D. Kidner, *Genesis* (Downers Grove: Inter-Varsity Press, 1967), pp. 15, 16, 178.

10

JOSEPH:

His Migration to Egypt
Genesis 37:1—41:57

For the tenth and final time, we now meet the phrase "These are the generations of . . ." (Gen. 37:2). It marks off the last main section of Genesis, a section that is 14 chapters in length (37–50). It focuses more on Joseph than on Jacob, more on Egypt than on Canaan.

We can most conveniently discuss the section in three separate segments: 37–41, 42–47, and 48–50. The time span of 37–41 is at least 20 years (see 37:2; 41:46; 41:53,54).

Joseph Sold into Slavery—37:1-36

At the age of 17, Joseph was helping his brothers in their task as shepherds. He worked along with all ten of his older brothers, but more specifically he assisted the four who were the sons of Bilhah and Zilpah (37:2; see 35:25,26). On at least one occasion, Joseph brought a bad report about them (doubtless all ten of them, as the later context indicates) back to his father Jacob.

Joseph and Benjamin, Jacob's eleventh and twelfth sons and

therefore his youngest sons, had been born to his favorite wife, Rachel. Benjamin, though younger than Joseph, was probably still only a small child at this time, a bit too young as yet to be Jacob's favorite. So of all his sons, Jacob preferred Joseph as one of the two sons who had been born when Jacob was an old man.

In recognition of Joseph's favored status, Jacob made for him a beautiful garment. We don't know exactly what it looked like, but it was probably either a "vari-colored tunic" (37:3)—the "coat of many colours" of the King James Version rendering—or a full-length robe, possibly with long sleeves. It was probably made of expensive materials and it was certainly a badge of honor. It was also a clear sign of favoritism, however, and it caused Joseph's brothers to become jealous of him (Gen. 37:4).

In the course of time, Joseph had two dreams that strained the relationship between himself and his brothers even further because he naively told them what he had dreamed.

The first dream portrayed all the brothers out in the fields at harvest time, tying up stalks of grain. Suddenly, Joseph's bundle stood upright and all the other bundles gathered around it and bowed down to it (37:7). The dream would, in fact, come true years later (see 42:6; 43:26; 44:14). But for now, Joseph's brothers were understandably indignant that the young Joseph implied that some day he would rule over them.

The second dream portrayed the sun, the moon and eleven stars bowing down to Joseph (Gen. 37:9). When Jacob heard about it, he scolded Joseph for implying that Jacob, Leah (Joseph's "mother" now that Rachel was dead; see 35:19), and Joseph's 11 brothers (including, of course, Benjamin) would eventually bow down to him (37:10). Jacob himself was to be pre-eminent (27:29), not Joseph—or at least so he thought!

Because of his dreams, Joseph's brothers now hated him all the more. But Jacob kept in mind what Joseph had said (37:11). Centuries later Mary, the virgin mother of Jesus, would demonstrate a similarly thoughtful response to the remarkable events surrounding the birth and boyhood of her firstborn son (see Luke 2:19,51).

Some time after Joseph had told his brothers about his dreams, they were grazing their father's flocks near Shechem. Jacob decided to send Joseph northward from the family estate at Hebron to find out how the men were getting along. When he got to Shechem, he was told that his brothers had moved the flocks farther north to the region near Dothan.

As soon as Joseph's brothers saw him coming in the distance, they began to make plans to kill him. They scornfully referred to him (Gen. 37:19) as "this dreamer" (literally, "master of dreams" or "dream expert"). Their intention was to kill him, throw him into a pit and claim that a wild animal had eaten him up.

But Reuben, Jacob's firstborn, felt responsible for Joseph's safety. He warned the other brothers not to take Joseph's life and told them to simply throw him into the pit. (He hoped to return later, rescue Joseph and take him back home to Jacob.) Many years later, when the tables had been turned and the brothers found themselves in an extremely difficult situation, Reuben would remind them of his earlier warning and would tell them that now they would all have to pay for their crime against Joseph (42:22).

When Joseph finally came to where his brothers were, they stripped him of his robe (37:23)—that hated symbol of parental favoritism (37:3)—and threw him into the pit (an empty water cistern). With callous indifference to his cries for help, they then sat down to have lunch.

As they did so, they spotted a caravan of Ishmaelites coming from Gilead and heading for Egypt. The camels in the caravan were loaded down with balm and other spices (37:25; Jer. 8:22 indicates that Gilead was noted for its balm). The Ishmaelites are also referred to in Genesis 37 as "Midianites" (37:28) and as "Medanites" (Hebrew text of 37:36). But this is not surprising in light of the fact that Midian and Medan were sons of Abraham through his concubine, Keturah (25:2), and were therefore half-brothers of Ishmael (see also Judg. 8:22,24,26).

Judah, reflecting on Reuben's warning (Gen. 37:22) not to shed Joseph's blood (37:26), suggested to his brothers that they sell Joseph to the Ishmaelites. After all, the brothers wouldn't want to have his blood on their hands, would they? Judah's proposal represents quite a contrast to Cain's insensitive attitude toward his brother Abel (see 4:9,10)!

The brothers agreed. They lifted Joseph from the pit and sold him to the Ishmaelites (37:28). The first "they" of 37:28 is the "brothers" of 37:27, according to Joseph's later statement in 45:4. (Stephen understood the story in the same way; see Acts 7:9.)

The price the brothers received was 20 shekels of silver (Gen. 37:28). That was still the monetary value of a male servant of Joseph's age in the time of Moses (Lev. 27:5). After selling Joseph, the brothers then left the area of the pit, as the context implies.

Reuben, meanwhile, had apparently been away tending the flocks while Joseph was being sold. When he returned to the pit (alone, perhaps to rescue Joseph; see Gen. 37:22), he was shocked to discover that Joseph wasn't there. So he tore his clothes as a sign of mourning (see 37:34) and then went to tell the other brothers (who, of course, already knew!).

The men dipped Joseph's robe in goat's blood and brought it back to their father Jacob. They cynically asked him whether it was Joseph's. Jacob identified it and came to the conclusion that a wild animal must have eaten Joseph up (37:33)—which is what most of the brothers had planned to tell Jacob anyhow (37:20)!

Jacob's response to the sight of that blood-spattered tunic was to tear his own clothes, put on sackcloth and mourn the loss of his son. His other sons and daughters tried to comfort him, but to no avail. The mention of Jacob's "daughters" (37:35) probably is intended to include daughters-in-law (see 38:2, as an example), since as far as we know, Jacob had only one daughter (see 30:21).

Jacob refused to be comforted and said that he would continue to mourn until he reached "Sheol," where his son was (37:35). The term *Sheol* is used in the Old Testament sometimes as a synonym for "grave." But it is also sometimes used as a more general reference to the "realm of the dead," the shadowy netherworld that served as a dwelling place for the deceased.

In line with the principle of progressive revelation, not every doctrine is fully developed or crystal clear in the Old Testament. God often revealed His truth in stages, one step at a time. The doctrine of immortality is an excellent case in point. It does not spring full-blown from the pages of the Old Testament, and for a very good reason. Only in the resurrection of Jesus Christ did immortality move from fond hope to glorious assurance. It was He "who abolished death, and brought life and immortality to light through the gospel" (2 Tim. 1:10)!

Jacob, whose understanding of the afterlife could only be partial, preferred mourning to being comforted. And even as he did so, his favorite son, Joseph, was being sold by the Ishmaelites to Potiphar, the Egyptian pharaoh's advisor and chief bodyguard (Gen. 37:36; see Ps. 105:17).

Genesis 37 is a story of naiveté and of latent pride on the part of Joseph. It is also a story of hatred, murderous intent and deception on the part of most of his brothers. In addition, favoritism and insensitivity on Jacob's part lurk in the background. They were undesirable qualities that brought him and his sons to grief, leading Jacob from joy to sorrow, Joseph from freedom to slavery and the brothers from contentment to jealous rage and violence.

And so it is with us. When we allow our emotions and desires to lead us into sinful acts (Jas. 1:14,15), we ourselves become miserable and everyone around us suffers.

The Judah-Tamar Episode—38:1-30

Genesis 38 forms a sad and sorry interlude in Joseph's story, just as Genesis 34 did in Jacob's story. Like Genesis 34, it tells a tale of lustful desire and its unfortunate consequences.

But Genesis 38 has a happy ending. It describes the birth of a boy who would continue the promised line of Abraham's descendants.

The position of Genesis 38 in the book as a whole indicates that its events occurred shortly after Jacob learned about Joseph's reputed death. Judah went to visit a man of Adullam (38:1), a town located southwest of Jerusalem. There Judah met and married a daughter of a man named Shua, a Canaanite. She bore him three sons (38:3-5), and in due course two of the boys reached marriageable age.

In accord with the custom of those times (see, for example, 21:21; 24:4), Judah chose a wife for his firstborn son, Er. The young man was wicked, however, and the Lord put him to death before his wife, Tamar, became pregnant.

Again in accord with ancient custom, Judah told his second son, Onan, to cohabit with Tamar, his deceased brother's widow. The purpose of such a practice was to produce offspring who could perpetuate the deceased man's name and estate.

For all practical purposes, Onan had no choice in the matter; it was his legal duty to do as Judah demanded (38:8; see especially Deut. 25:5,6, a passage referred to in Matt. 22:24). The custom itself is known as "levirate marriage" (the Latin word *levir* means "brother-in-law") and explains why Boaz had to get legal permission from Naomi's and Ruth's nearest male relative before Boaz himself, next in line, could marry the widow Ruth (see Ruth 3:12,13; 4:1-6).

Onan, however, knew that Tamar's offspring wouldn't be his own. So he spilled his semen on the ground when he lay with her. His action displeased the Lord, who then put Onan to death also (Gen. 38:9,10).

Just as the sinfulness of the men of Sodom (see 19:4-9) gave rise to the word "sodomy" (a synonym for "homosexuality"), so also Onan's sin gave rise to the word "onanism," a synonym for "coitus interruptus" (now widely used as a means of birth control). But the Lord slew Onan not simply for practicing coitus interruptus. He did so because Onan refused to perform his levirate duty and continue Judah's line.

After Onan's death, Judah told Tamar to go back to her father's house and live there as a widow until Shelah, Judah's third son, reached marriageable age. Actually, Judah had no intention of giving Shelah to Tamar as a husband. Directly or indirectly, she had caused the death of Judah's first two sons, and he was afraid that Shelah also might die because of her (38:11,14).

Some time later, Judah decided to go to Timnah (a place of uncertain location) to shear his sheep. His wife had recently died and the period of mourning for her was over (38:12).

When Tamar heard that Judah was going to Timnah, she took off her widow's clothes and dressed herself like a prostitute (see Prov. 7:10), including covering her face with a veil to avoid recognition. She then stationed herself at a certain place on the road (Gen. 38:14), apparently a customary procedure for prostitutes in ancient times (see Jer. 3:2). She obviously intended to prey on Judah's loneliness and weakness for her own ends, however commendable they might have been.

When Judah, en route to Timnah, saw her, he was overpowered by his own desires and agreed to pay her a young goat

112

in exchange for her services (Gen. 38:17). He didn't recognize her, of course, because the veil concealed her identity. She demanded collateral until a goat could be sent to her. The collateral in this case consisted of Judah's personal cylinder seal[1] which he used to sign and seal documents, the cord on which it hung from his neck, and his personal walking stick (38:18).

Judah agreed to her terms and cohabited with her, after which she left the area and changed back into her widow's clothes. When Judah later sent his Adullamite friend with the goat in order to retrieve his personal items, the woman was nowhere to be found. So Judah decided to simply drop the matter (38:20-23).

But about three months later, Judah's affair with the "prostitute" returned to haunt him. He learned that his daughter-in-law Tamar had become illegitimately pregnant. Later Mosaic punishment for extramarital intercourse was death by stoning (Deut. 22:20-24; see also John 8:4,5), although in certain cases being burned to death was the prescribed penalty (Lev. 21:9). Judah ordered the latter for Tamar.

When she was led out for formal sentencing and execution, however, she brought with her Judah's seal, cord and walking stick, claiming them to be the possessions of the man who had made her pregnant. Judah recognized them immediately and then praised Tamar for being more righteous than he was. He conceded that Tamar's present condition was all his fault, since she had been reduced to a desperate course of action to protect Er's inheritance simply because Judah wouldn't allow the now-fully-grown Shelah to enter into levirate marriage with her (Gen. 38:26).

The time of Tamar's delivery eventually arrived. Like Rebekah, Er's great-grandmother, Tamar also gave birth to twin boys (see 25:21-24). As she was about to deliver, one of the twins reached out his hand, so the attending midwife tied a scarlet thread around it to mark him as the firstborn (38:28). But he withdrew his hand back into the womb, and then his brother was born ahead of him. The surprised midwife said, in effect, "You have really broken through on your own!" That's why the boy was named *Perez*, which means "breaking through."

The baby with the scarlet thread on his hand was then born.

He was named *Zerah,* the meaning of which is uncertain. It has been related by some scholars to a similar word meaning "sunrise," from which "scarlet" has been deduced, and by others to a word meaning "braided," from which "thread" has been deduced.

Though born of an adulterous relationship, Perez became the ancestor of David (Ruth 4:18-22) who in turn became the ancestor of Jesus Christ (see especially Matt. 1:1-6). God truly works in mysterious ways to further His own purposes, and even the results of sinful desire can be used by Him to perform His perfect will (Exod. 9:15,16; Ps. 76:10).

Joseph Employed and Imprisoned—39:1—40:23

The scene now shifts back to Egypt, and the first verse of Genesis 39 reviews the information found in the last verse of Genesis 37 in order to get us back on the track of Joseph's story. We are reminded again that Joseph had become a servant of Potiphar, a high Egyptian official.

Genesis 39 stresses the fact that God was with Joseph (39:2,3,21,23), an emphasis noted by Stephen in his review of Israel's history (see Acts 7:9). Joseph's master observed that fact as well (Gen. 39:3), just as Abimelech had done in Abraham's case (21:22) and a later Abimelech had done in Isaac's case (26:28).

Everything Joseph did was successful (39:3). He may have been the prototype of the righteous man described in Psalm 1:3. The Lord blessed the Egyptian official's household for Joseph's sake (Gen. 39:5), as He had blessed Laban for Jacob's sake (30:27). In summary, Joseph's master learned that he could entrust anything to him, so he put everything he owned in Joseph's care (39:6). But Joseph possessed even more than spiritual qualities and administrative abilities. He was also handsome and well-built (39:6)—so much so that his master's wife "lifted up her eyes" at him (see 39:7 *NASB* margin). That ancient phrase meant "to look with desire or lust," as our context demonstrates and as Section 25 of Hammurabi's famous code of laws shows (see chap. 1).[2]

The woman asked Joseph to come to bed with her, but he refused. He told her that to do so would be to betray his master's trust and confidence in him. And he informed her also that if he did what she wanted him to do, he would be sinning against God Himself (39:9).

A very important theological point is being made here: our sin is never private. Every time we sin, we sin against God. And, in a certain sense, our sin is always against Him alone (Ps. 51:4).

The woman was persistent, however. Finally one day, when no one else was around, she grabbed Joseph by the clothes and again begged him to come to bed with her. But he wisely left his clothes in her hand and ran away (Gen. 39:12). One of the best ways for us to keep from sinning is to flee from temptation whenever it begins to work on us (2 Tim. 2:22).

Angry by now, the woman called out to the men of her household. She told them Joseph had tried to rape her (Gen. 39:14) and she showed them his clothing as proof of her claim! She referred to him as a "Hebrew," a term of reproach when used by an Egyptian. When her husband returned home she told him the same story, this time demeaning Joseph even further by calling him a "Hebrew slave" (39:17).

Potiphar, understandably enraged, put Joseph into the prison house where the pharaoh's prisoners were held (39:20). But once again the Lord was with Joseph and blessed him. God gave him favor in the sight of the prison warden, who in turn gave him important responsibilities even while he was in jail. The warden placed the same kind of confidence in Joseph that his former master had placed in him. Joseph was a worthy son of Jacob; the Lord was with both men wherever they went (see 28:15).

While Joseph was in prison, the pharaoh's chief cupbearer and chief baker wronged or offended the pharaoh in some way. So the men were arrested and turned over to Potiphar, who put them in the same prison where Joseph was confined.

Joseph was assigned to be their servant (40:1-4). After the two new prisoners had been in custody for some time, one night each of them had a dream.

The next morning, Joseph could tell by looking at their faces that they were dejected (40:6,7; see also 41:8). Joseph asked them what was wrong and they said that they had had dreams but that there was no one available to interpret them (Gen. 40:8). Belief in the importance of having significant dreams interpreted was widespread in the countries of the ancient Near East.[3]

Joseph told the men that only God can interpret dreams properly and precisely. He would say much the same thing to the pharaoh two years later (41:16,25,28), and Daniel would speak in a similar way to Nebuchadnezzar of Babylon (Dan. 2:27,28). The careers of Joseph and Daniel, God's men who eventually came to occupy prominent positions in foreign courts, were very much alike, even though separated by hundreds of years.

Joseph asked the pharaoh's officials to describe their dreams. After the cupbearer had spoken, Joseph interpreted his dream for him (Gen. 40:12,13). In the light of what Joseph had said earlier (40:8), his interpretation implied that he was attuned to God's wisdom. Within three days, Joseph said, the pharaoh would lift up the head of the cupbearer and restore him to his former position. To "lift up the head" in that context meant to "graciously release from prison," as a comparison of Jeremiah 52:31 and 2 Kings 25:27 shows.

Then Joseph requested that the cupbearer put in a good word for him to the pharaoh. After all, Joseph had already been subjected to the indignities of being kidnapped, sold as a slave and imprisoned even though innocent (Gen. 40:14,15).

Next, the baker described his dream, which Joseph interpreted. Within three days, Joseph said, the pharaoh would lift up the head of the baker. Up to that point the interpretation of the baker's dream was the same as that of the cupbearer's dream. But now to "lift up the head" took on ominous tones; it meant, in the baker's case, to "behead"! The baker, said Joseph, would be beheaded and then his body would be impaled on a stake as a warning to others who might be plotting crimes against the pharaoh (40:18,19). (Ancient drawings and inscriptions indicate that "impale on a stake" is the most likely meaning of the phrase "hang on a tree" in the Old Testament.)

Since God had given Joseph the interpretations they both came true as predicted. The third day was the pharaoh's birthday, so he threw a party for all his servants (40:20). The chief cupbearer was restored to his former position and the chief baker was beheaded.

The chief cupbearer, back on the job, was so happy that he completely failed to remember Joseph's request. Genesis 40 ends

116

with the simple, sad observation that the cupbearer "forgot him."

But God didn't forget—and two years later Joseph's seemingly hopeless situation would be totally and miraculously changed.

Joseph Exalted—41:1-57

After those two full years had passed, the pharaoh himself had a couple of disturbing dreams. In the first dream he watched as seven ugly, emaciated cows devoured seven sleek, fat cows. In the second he saw seven thin, scorched heads of grain swallowing up seven full, healthy heads of grain (Gen. 41:1-7).

The next morning, the pharaoh's mind was troubled by what he had dreamed. As in the case of his chief cupbearer and chief baker (40:6), the pharaoh was worried because he didn't know what his dreams meant (see also Dan. 2:1,3). Worst of all, the sorcerers and wise men of Egypt couldn't interpret them either (Gen. 41:8; see also Dan. 2:8-11). Egyptian sorcerers were intelligent and clever (Exod. 7:11,22; 8:7), but there were some things even *they* couldn't do (Exod. 8:18)!

The unusual flurry of activity in the pharaoh's court finally jogged the memory of the chief cupbearer. He apologized to the pharaoh for not telling him about the "Hebrew youth" who had correctly interpreted two other dreams two years earlier (Gen. 41:9-13).

So the pharaoh sent for Joseph (see Ps. 105:20), who shaved himself and changed his clothes before coming into the pharaoh's presence (Gen. 41:14). When the pharaoh asked him if he had the ability to interpret dreams, Joseph said that he couldn't possibly do so apart from God's help (41:16; see also 40:8; Dan. 2:27,28,30).

Joseph's complete dependence on God was one of his most admirable characteristics. We, too, should always recognize and acknowledge that all we are and have comes from God (2 Cor. 3:5).

When he described his dreams to Joseph, the pharaoh added a detail or two that we hadn't been informed about before. He said that the emaciated cows looked worse than anything he had ever seen in his life (Gen. 41:19). He also said that even after they had devoured the fat cows, they were still as emaciated as before (41:21). Although the pharaoh didn't yet know what his dreams meant, he obviously sensed that something terrible was about to happen!

Joseph then told the pharaoh that his two dreams had only one meaning: seven years of great abundance would be followed by seven years of severe famine throughout the whole land of Egypt. Such seven-year famines were not uncommon elsewhere (see 2 Kings 8:1), but they almost never occurred in Egypt because of the dependable regularity of the annual overflow of the waters of the Nile river. Rare examples of lengthy famines were not entirely unknown in Egypt, however.[4]

Joseph went on to tell the pharaoh that his dream had been repeated in two forms because the matter had been determined by God and because God would waste no time in bringing it to pass (Gen. 41:32).

Joseph recommended that the pharaoh put a wise and intelligent man in charge of Egypt to oversee the storage of surplus food during the years of abundance so the people wouldn't starve during the years of famine.

The pharaoh readily agreed to Joseph's proposal. In fact, he decided that Joseph himself should be that man (see Acts 7:10), since it was quite obvious that Joseph possessed "a divine spirit" (Gen. 41:38). It is possible also to translate that phrase "the Spirit of God," but such a translation would be out of character in a statement coming from the lips of a pagan, polytheistic ruler. (The same observation applies to the similar phrases found in Dan. 4:8,9,18; 5:11,14.)

So the pharaoh formally appointed Joseph to be second in command throughout Egypt (Gen. 41:40; see also Ps. 105:21,22). Joseph would ride in a chariot second only to that of the pharaoh himself (Gen. 41:43); he would wear the pharaoh's personal signet ring (see also Esther 3:10); he would be dressed in the finest clothing (see also Esther 6:11); and he would wear a gold chain around his neck (see also Dan. 5:7,16,29). The pharaoh would make sure that Joseph had all the trappings of royalty, including the homage of the people, who were required to stand at attention whenever Joseph made his appearance (Gen. 41:43).[5]

We don't know who this pharaoh was. But if our rough chronology is correct (see chap. 1), he would have been one of the early Hyksos rulers. The *Hyksos* (a word meaning "rulers of foreign lands") were Asian Semites who conquered Egypt c. 1785 B.C. and ruled there till about 1550 B.C., when they were driven out by native Egyptians.

The Hyksos period in Egypt is often called the "Second Intermediate Period" of Egyptian history and included Dynasties XIII through XVII. The fact that the Hyksos were Semites helps to explain, humanly speaking, why Joseph gained such a relatively favorable reception from the authorities when he arrived in Egypt, since Joseph himself was a Semite. Such an explanation in no way detracts from the reality of God's providence in Joseph's life, of course. If correct, it simply serves as yet another illustration of how God uses people and events to further His gracious purposes in the lives of His children.

Now 30 years old (Gen. 41:46), Joseph had lived in Egypt for 13 years (see 37:2) by the time he became second in command in that land. Seven years of abundance came, just as he had predicted. During those years his wife Asenath bore him two sons (41:50-52). The firstborn was named *Manasseh* ("he causes to forget") because God had made Joseph "forget" all his previous loneliness and misery. The second son was named *Ephraim* ("twice fruitful") because God had made Joseph "fruitful" in the land of his distress. Implied also in the name is the fact that God had given Joseph "two" sons (see 41:50).

Again as Joseph had predicted, the seven abundant years ended and were followed by seven years of famine (41:54; see also Acts 7:11). Joseph's foresight, however, made it possible for Egypt to feed not only its own people (41:55,56) but also the people from all the surrounding regions (41:57).

Genesis 37—41 has told us the story of how God was with Joseph and of how He made him prosperous in everything he did. Joseph found favor in the eyes of his father (37:3), in the eyes of Potiphar (39:4), in the eyes of the prison warden (39:21) and in the eyes of the pharaoh himself (41:38).

And in everything that happened, God's perfect plan was at work to fulfill His purposes in the lives of Joseph, his brothers and his father Jacob.

Footnotes

1. See, for example, J. A. Thompson, *The Bible and Archaeology*, revised edition (Grand Rapids: Wm. B. Eerdmans Publishing Co., 1972), pp. 26, 32.

2. See T. J. Meek in J. B. Pritchard, editor, *Ancient Near Eastern Texts*, second edition (Princeton: Princeton University Press, 1955), p. 167.

3. See especially A. Leo Oppenheim in *Transactions of the American Philosophical Society*, Volume 46, Part 3 (1956), pp. 179-373.

4. See J. A. Wilson in Pritchard, editor, *Ancient Near Eastern Texts*, pp. 31, 32.

5. See T. O. Lambdin in *Journal of the American Oriental Society* 73 (July-September, 1953), p. 146.

11

JACOB:
His Migration to Egypt
Genesis 42:1—47:31

Genesis 37—41 describes how and why Joseph went down to Egypt and Genesis 42—47 tells us how and why Jacob did the same.

Neither man went willingly. Joseph was sold into slavery and then imprisoned, rising to prominence only later. Jacob went to Egypt only after a long and complex series of events compelled him to make the move.

But it is those events that give Genesis 42—47 its drama and suspense and that make it one of the most absorbing sections in all of Genesis.

Jacob's Sons Go to Egypt During the Famine—42:1—44:34

The same famine that had struck Egypt had also descended on the neighboring territories, including Canaan. When Jacob learned that there was grain available in Egypt, he told his 11 sons to stop staring at each other and to go to Egypt in order to buy some food. Only in that way would the family be able to remain alive.

Jacob permitted only 10 of the brothers to make the trip. He didn't want to send Benjamin along because he was afraid that harm might overtake him (Gen. 42:4). After all, Joseph and Benjamin were the only two sons that Rachel had borne to Jacob. And since Rachel, now dead, had been Jacob's favorite wife, he didn't want to lose Benjamin as he had lost Joseph.

Unknown to Jacob and his family, Joseph had become a high official in Egypt (42:6), second only to the pharaoh himself (41:40,43). So when the brothers arrived in Egypt, they were obliged to buy grain directly from Joseph. They also had to bow down to him (42:6)—just as he had dreamed that they would some day (37:7,9)!

Joseph had been a teen-ager when his brothers had last seen him (37:2). He was now at least 37 years old (41:46,53,54), wearing Egyptian clothes, speaking the Egyptian language (42:23) and in a position of authority, so his brothers didn't recognize him (42:8). But they had already become adults when he had last seen them. Their appearance had evidently not changed much, because he recognized them immediately (42:7).

Remembering the dreams he had had (42:9), Joseph at first treated his brothers harshly. He pretended not to know them, accused them of being spies and put them all in prison for three days (42:7-17). Twenty years or more earlier he had described his dreams to his brothers and they had scoffed at the possibility that he would some day rule over them (37:8). But now here they were, calling him "my lord" and referring to themselves as his "servants" (42:10)!

On the third day of their imprisonment, Joseph went to see his brothers. He told them he was going to keep one of them in jail until the others had gone back home and brought their youngest brother to Egypt.

The brothers came to the conclusion that their present calamity was the result of the sin they had committed against Joseph so many years before (42:21). Reuben then reminded them that he had warned them not to harm Joseph but that they had failed to listen to him (42:22; see 37:21,22).

As they discussed their plight, Joseph was listening to what they said. But they didn't know he could understand them because they thought he was an Egyptian. After all, he had been using an interpreter (42:23).

The entire scene, however, was too much for Joseph. He left the room to weep and release his pent-up emotions. Then he came back and bound Simeon as the others watched (42:24). Although Simeon was Jacob's second son, Joseph bound him instead of Reuben, Jacob's firstborn, probably because Reuben had earlier tried to save Joseph (37:21,22).

After Simeon had been locked up in the prison, Joseph gave his men orders to fill the grain sacks of the other brothers. His men were also told to put each brother's money back in his sack and then to send them on their way to Canaan.

When the brothers stopped for the night and one of them opened his sack to get feed for his donkey, he saw his money and immediately told the others. They trembled at the sight of it, wondering what in the world God was doing to them!

After they arrived in Canaan, the brothers told their father Jacob the whole story. Then when the other sacks were opened and each man's money was found in his sack, the men were frightened all the more.

Jacob, who had already mourned the loss of Joseph and had now lost Simeon as well, didn't want the other brothers to take Benjamin to Egypt. Even Reuben's generous offer of his own two sons as collateral for Benjamin's safety (42:36-38) didn't change Jacob's mind. He was still afraid, as he had been earlier (42:4), that harm would come to Benjamin. And if that should happen, he was sure the other brothers would be guilty of sending their father to an early grave because he would grieve over his youngest son (42:38; see also 37:35).

But the famine became more and more severe, so when Jacob and his family had used up all the grain the brothers had brought from Egypt he again told his sons to go back there for more food (43:2). Judah said they were willing to go but only if Jacob would agree to send Benjamin along, since otherwise the trip would be of no avail.

This time, Judah offered himself as collateral, assuring Jacob that he would take full responsibility for Benjamin's safety (43:9). Judah stated that if Benjamin didn't accompany the others to Egypt the whole family—Jacob, his children and his grandchildren—would die of hunger (43:8).

We observe that Judah, Jacob's fourth son, had now become

123

the spokesman for all the brothers. He had begun to assume that role many years earlier (37:26,27), and he would continue to speak for his brothers in the future as well (44:14-34; 46:28). Judah's tribe would eventually become pre-eminent among the 12 tribes of Israel (see 49:8-12), and he himself would be an ancestor of the Messiah (Matt. 1:2; Luke 3:33).

Judah's persuasive arguments finally convinced Jacob to allow his sons to return to Egypt and take Benjamin with them. He advised them to take samples of some of the best products of Canaan as gifts for the Egyptian official. He also told them to take twice as much money as they needed. If they did so they would be able to return the money they had found in their sacks—money which, Jacob hoped, had been put there by mistake (Gen. 43:12).

Jacob prayed that God Almighty, the God of the patriarchs (17:1; 28:3; 35:11; see especially Exod. 6:3), would exert His power and grant Jacob's sons mercy in the official's eyes (Gen. 43:14). In any event, Jacob was resigned to his fate: "If I am bereaved . . . , I am bereaved" (43:14).

After the brothers arrived in Egypt and Joseph saw that Benjamin was with them, he ordered his steward to prepare a feast. When the steward took the men to Joseph's house they were afraid that it was because of the money they had found in their sacks. They felt that now they would be enslaved and their donkeys would be confiscated. So they took the steward aside and explained to him that they had brought back the money found in their sacks. They further told him that they had brought other money also with which to buy food (Gen. 43:19-22).

The steward assured them that there was no need to worry. He told them that their God must have put the money in their sacks since he himself had received money for the food they had bought earlier. Simeon was then released from prison and all the brothers were provided with the same kind of hospitality for themselves and their animals (43:24) that Laban had given to Abraham's servant and animals so many years before (24:32).

When Joseph came into the house, the brothers brought their gift to him. Once more they bowed down before him (43:26), as they would do later on as well (43:28)—fulfilling Joseph's earlier dream again and again (37:7,9)!

124

Joseph inquired about the health of their father and then took a closer look at Benjamin. The narrator at this point has emphasized the special status of Benjamin by referring to him as "his [that is, Joseph's] mother's son" (43:29). Joseph said to Benjamin, "May God be gracious to you" (43:29). The essence of that phrase would become well known and loved in benedictions and prayers of later years (Num. 6:25; Ps. 67:1).

Once again, the experience was beyond Joseph's powers of self-control. His heart was so stirred by the sight of his brother Benjamin that he left the room to weep (Gen. 43:30). If Jeremiah can justly be called the "weeping prophet," surely Joseph can justly be called the "weeping patriarch" (see 42:24; 45:2,14,15; 46:29)! He must have been a very tenderhearted and sensitive person.

After washing his face and regaining control of his emotions (43:31)—something he wasn't always successful in doing (45:1)—he returned and ordered food to be brought in. He was served in one place and his brothers in another place. His Egyptian guests were served in still another place because Egyptians would not eat together with Hebrews, perhaps for ritual reasons (43:32; see also Exod. 8:26). The Egyptian avoidance of shepherds (Gen. 46:34), on the other hand, was probably not for ritual but for social reasons.

As the brothers were being given places at the table in the correct order of their ages, from the oldest to the youngest, they looked at each other in amazement, wondering how an Egyptian official could possibly know who was who (43:33)! Portions of food were then distributed to them from Joseph's table with Benjamin receiving five times as much as any of the others (43:34; see also 45:22).

After the meal, Joseph told his steward to fill up his visitors' sacks with food, put each man's money back into his sack and put Joseph's own silver cup into Benjamin's sack. The brothers were then escorted out of the city the next morning. If Joseph served under one of the Hyksos rulers, as seems quite likely (see chap. 10), the city mentioned in 44:4,13 was probably their capital, Avaris. Its exact location is still somewhat uncertain, although it would have been located in Egypt's eastern delta region.[1]

When the men had gone only a short distance from the city, Joseph sent his steward to overtake them and accuse them of repaying good with evil by stealing his silver cup. The steward caught up with them and repeated Joseph's words to them (44:4-6).

Not knowing that the cup was in Benjamin's sack, the brothers said indignantly, "With whomever of your servants it is found, let him die, and we also will be my lord's slaves" (44:9). Their retort was similar to what Jacob, equally unsuspecting, had said years before to Laban concerning the latter's household idols (31:32).

The steward agreed to the men's proposal but he softened the potential penalty to slavery for the guilty brother and freedom for the others (44:10). The suspense of the story builds as we read that the sacks were searched, beginning with the one belonging to the oldest and ending with the one belonging to the youngest. And there, of course, in Benjamin's sack, as previously planned by Joseph, the silver cup was found. The brothers, sensing that all was now lost, tore their clothes as a sign of mourning and despair (44:13; see also 37:29,34) and went back to Avaris with the steward.

When the men arrived at Joseph's house, they threw themselves to the ground before him (44:14), again in fulfillment of his earlier dream (37:7,9). Joseph—doubtless with tongue in cheek—asked them how they could possibly have expected to trick a man with the occult powers that he possessed (44:15)!

Judah once again became the spokesman for the others (see 43:3). He readily admitted their collective guilt and indicated that they would all resign themselves to becoming Joseph's slaves (44:16). But Joseph responded as his steward had: only Benjamin would become Joseph's servant, and the others were free to go back to their father.

At this point in the story, Judah made one of the most eloquent pleas to be found anywhere in the Bible (44:18-34). Consistently referring to Joseph as "my lord" and to himself, his brothers and their father as "your servant(s)" (once again, see 37:8!), Judah begged Joseph for a hearing and continued by reviewing the entire affair in a highly emotional way.

He praised Joseph by claiming him to be like the pharaoh himself (44:18). He pointed out that Benjamin was the only one of his mother's sons left and was therefore beloved by his father (44:20). He asserted that Jacob had already lost one of his wife's two sons and would die heartbroken if he lost the other (44:27-29). Employing the same Hebrew phrase that would later be used of David's relationship to Jonathan (see 1 Sam. 18:1), Judah indicated that Jacob's life was bound up in Benjamin's life so completely that the loss of Benjamin would kill Jacob and the brothers would then be responsible (Gen. 44:30,31).

Finally, Judah pleaded with Joseph to enslave him rather than Benjamin (44:33). He said that he couldn't possibly go back to his father unless he took Benjamin with him because he couldn't bear to see the misery and despair that would overcome Jacob.

And so Judah ended his earnest request by offering himself as a substitute for his brother. Are we not reminded of an infinitely greater offering, nearly two thousand years later, by an infinitely greater Substitute (John 10:11-18)?

The Brothers Are Reconciled to Joseph—45:1-28

By this time Joseph had seen so much remorse and repentance and unselfishness in his brothers that he could no longer control his own emotions (Gen. 45:1; see 43:31). So he sent all the other people out of the room and then revealed his identity to his brothers (45:1; Acts 7:13). His joyful sobbing was so loud that Egyptians in other sections of the palace could hear it!

Joseph exclaimed to his brothers, "I am Joseph!"

But they were so surprised at hearing him speak to them in their own language and they were so afraid at learning that he was still alive that they were unable to answer him (Gen. 45:3). They had not seen Joseph for 22 years (see 37:2; 41:46,53; 45:6), so they probably thought that by now he had died in slavery. Seeing him alive was quite a shock to them.

So Joseph tried to reassure them and calm their fears. This time he said, "I am *your brother* Joseph" (45:4, italics added), stressing the fact that from his own standpoint, at least, he still cherished that brotherly relationship. He didn't overlook the fact that it was they who had sold him into slavery in Egypt, of course. But he emphasized God's sovereign will behind what had taken place (45:5,7,8). Because God had made Joseph the pharaoh's advisor, Jacob's entire family would now be saved

127

from starvation! (Stephen stressed that point also; see Acts 7:9,10.)

Joseph then told his brothers to hurry back home and bring his father and the rest of the clan to Egypt right away. Again, the narrator stresses God's hand in Joseph's rise to power (Gen. 45:9). On their arrival, Jacob and his family would be settled in Goshen (45:10) in the eastern delta, the best part of the land of Egypt (45:18), and all their needs would be cared for.

Apparently noticing their reluctance to believe him, Joseph again assured them of his identity. He reminded them that he was speaking to them in their own language, not through an interpreter (45:12). After repeating his desire that they hurry on to Canaan and bring Jacob and the other members of the family back as soon as possible, he enjoyed a tearful reunion with Benjamin and then with his other brothers.

When the pharaoh learned that Joseph's brothers had come to Egypt, he was delighted. He told Joseph to order his brothers to take carts full of supplies with them to Canaan. They were then to bring Jacob and their families back to Egypt.

The pharaoh's command underscored what by now had become Joseph's fondest desire. Jacob's entire clan would be reunited once again! The pharaoh's promise that they would eat "the fat of the land" (45:18) was reminiscent of Isaac's blessing on Jacob (see 27:28) and should be viewed as at least a partial fulfillment of it.

Jacob's sons agreed to Joseph's proposal. Among the supplies Joseph gave to each of them was an outfit of clothes. To Benjamin, however, Joseph gave five outfits (45:22; see also 43:34) as well as an additional present of 300 shekels of silver. Plenty of other provisions were sent along with them also. As they departed, Joseph, with a twinkle in his eye, told them not to fight or quarrel with each other during the trip (45:24). He knew his brothers' weaknesses all too well!

After the men had arrived at their father's home, Jacob listened to their story in stunned disbelief. But when they told him everything Joseph had said, and when he saw the carts Joseph had sent, his spirit revived. Now convinced that Joseph was still alive, he determined to make the long journey to Egypt. "I will go and see him," he said, "before I die" (45:28).

The Whole Family Moves to Egypt and Settles There—46:1—47:31

Jacob was apparently living on the patriarchal estate at Hebron at this time (see 35:27). So his trip to Egypt took him and his family westward to Beersheba, where he stopped briefly in order to worship the Lord (46:1) as his father Isaac (26:23-25) and grandfather Abraham (21:33) had done before him.

While at Beersheba, Jacob had a night vision similar to that of Isaac in the same place years earlier. Even the words that God spoke to each man were similar (see 26:24; 46:3). The Lord spoke Jacob's name twice, expressing the same sense of urgency as he had to Abraham at Moriah and eliciting the same response: "Here I am" (46:2; see 22:11).

God told Jacob not to be afraid. He said that it was His will for Jacob and his family to go down to Egypt, because there God would make of him a great nation (46:3). The Lord's prophecy would be abundantly fulfilled (Exod. 1:7)!

God also promised to accompany Jacob to Egypt and to bring him (in the person of his descendants) back to Canaan again (Gen. 46:4)—a prediction of the exodus (see also 15:16)! The Lord's promise to be with Jacob at all times had first been spoken many years earlier at Bethel (28:15) and had followed him throughout his life (31:3). A final promise to Jacob was that the hand of his own son, Joseph, would close Jacob's eyes at the time of his death (46:4).

After the divine confirmation of his decision to visit Joseph, Jacob set out westward from Beersheba with his family, his cattle and his goods, eventually arriving in Egypt (46:5-7).

Genesis 46:8-27 is another section of "connective tissue" (see 22:20-24; 25:12-18; 36:1-43). In this case, however, the genealogy is very interesting in its own right.

A question immediately arises: how is the number "seventy" (46:27; see also Exod. 1:5; Deut. 10:22) to be understood? The section itself demands a literal understanding of the number, since 33 (Gen. 46:15) plus 16 (46:18) plus 14 (46:22) plus 7 (46:25) equals 70.

And now we face a second question: how does the "seventy" of 46:27 relate to the "sixty-six" of 46:26?

Let's attempt a reconstruction based on the data before us.

129

One problem is that the number of names in 46:8-15 is 34, not 33. We can't exclude the name of Jacob's daughter Dinah (46:15) because the text explicitly states that 33 was the total of "his sons and his daughters" listed here, and Dinah's name is the only clearly female name in the list. The only other possibility readily available for exclusion is the name "Ohad" (46:10), which does not appear in the parallel lists in Numbers 26:12-14 or 1 Chronicles 4:24. Although "Ohad" does appear also in Exodus 6:15, both there and in Genesis 46:10 its Hebrew form looks very much like that of the nearby name "Zohar." Perhaps, then, "Ohad" was added accidentally by a scribe while he was engaged in copying the text. As a comparison of Genesis 46:8-25 and Numbers 26:4-57, for example, will demonstrate, scribal omissions, additions, variations in spelling and so forth are rather frequent in genealogical lists.

Another problem is the fact that although the names of Er and Onan were included in the total listing of 70, those two men had already died in Canaan (Gen. 46:12). We observe, however, that 46:26 states that "all the persons belonging to Jacob, *who came to Egypt*, his direct descendants, not including the wives of Jacob's sons, were sixty-six persons in all." So from the total of 70 we must subtract the names of Er and Onan—and we must also subtract the names of Manasseh and Ephraim, Joseph's sons who had been *born* in Egypt (46:20,27).

The "seventy" of 46:27, then, is the ideal, complete number of Jacob's descendants who would have been in Egypt if Er and Onan had not sinned and been punished with death (38:7-10).

(Jacob himself can't be included in enumerating the 70, since Exodus 1:5 clearly states that it was his *offspring* who numbered 70. The figure of 75 given in Stephen's speech in Acts 7:14 includes additional sons of Joseph, presumably born after Jacob's arrival in Egypt. In fact, the Greek translation of the Old Testament that Stephen was perhaps quoting from reads "75" in both Genesis 46:27 and Exodus 1:5.)

Other reconstructions of who it was that constituted the 70 members of Jacob's family who arrived in Egypt at one time or another have been attempted, of course. But the one outlined above seems to account best for all the textual evidence that we have.

130

When Jacob reached the Egyptian frontier, he sent Judah ahead of him to lead the way to Goshen (Gen. 46:28). Again Judah's importance is emphasized by the narrator, as we observed earlier (see 37:26,27; 43:3-10; 44:14-34). After the family had arrived in Goshen, Joseph came out in his chariot to meet his father (46:29). The mention of the chariot (see also 41:43; 50:9) is another indication of the likelihood that Joseph went down to Egypt during the Hyksos period, since chariots were not used in Egypt until the time of the Hyksos conquest.

The meeting between Joseph and Jacob was highly charged emotionally (46:29). Jacob's lonely years had ended and he declared that he was ready to die.

But Joseph apparently felt that everyone still had a lot of living to do! He told Jacob's family that he would now announce their arrival to the pharaoh and forewarn him that they were shepherds by trade. For their part, they were advised to tell the pharaoh that shepherding was a long and honorable tradition in their family. Only then would they be able to settle down in Goshen, because the Egyptians tended to look down their noses at shepherds. Under ordinary circumstances, in fact, they simply refused to associate with them (46:34).

Joseph then went in and made the announcement to the pharaoh, introducing five of his brothers to him. The pharaoh told Joseph to allow Jacob and his family to live in Goshen, the best part of the land. Furthermore, the most able men among them were to be put in charge of the pharaoh's livestock (47:1-6). Even in times of economic instability there are usually worthwhile tasks for able people to perform.

When Joseph introduced his father Jacob to the pharaoh, the pharaoh asked him how old he was. Jacob replied that his wanderings had so far lasted for only a few miserable years—a mere 130, to be exact (47:9)! They had been brief, he continued, in comparison to those of his forefathers. (Abraham, after all, had lived for 175 years, Isaac for 180; see 25:7; 35:28.) Again we observe the patriarchs' evaluation of themselves as wanderers, strangers, exiles (see also Heb. 11:13).

Jacob "blessed" the pharaoh at the beginning and the end of their conversation (Gen. 47:7,10). But that probably means no more than that he said "hello" and "goodbye" to him. The

Hebrew word *shalom* (literally "wholeness," "well-being," "peace") is universally used in the same sense today.

And so it was that Joseph settled his father and brothers in Goshen, called "the field of Zoan" in Psalm 78:12,43 and "the land of Rameses" in Genesis 47:11 (see also Exod. 1:11). If the "Rameses" mentioned was Rameses II, who ruled Egypt centuries after Joseph's time, the reference to the land of Rameses in Genesis 47:11 could possibly be a later editorial touch.

As the famine continued and became more and more severe, the Egyptians finally used up all their money to buy the grain that Joseph had stored up during the years of abundance (47:13-15). They soon found it necessary to trade their cattle for Joseph's grain (47:16,17), then their lands and finally themselves (47:18-20). In this way all the land in Egypt became in fact what it had always been in theory: the personal property of the pharaoh. Only the land that belonged to the priests was not turned over to the pharaoh. He had traditionally given them a regular allowance to live on, so they didn't have to exchange their land for grain (47:22,26).

Genesis 47:21 presents something of a problem to the reader, but it seems to mean that the Egyptian people were ordered to move into the towns temporarily until seed for planting could be efficiently distributed to them (47:23). They were then to plant the seed on the pharaoh's land, and when the harvest came in they were to give one-fifth of it to the pharaoh and keep four-fifths for themselves and their households (47:24,25). This was simply an extension of a practice that had already begun in an initial way during the seven years of abundance (41:34). The difference was that during the abundant years the people had continued to own their own land, while now all the land belonged to the pharaoh by legal statute (47:26).

Meanwhile Jacob's family, soon to become the people of Israel, continued to live in Goshen. There they became wealthy and increased their numbers by leaps and bounds (47:27), just as God promised they would (46:3; see also Exod. 1:7). The "people" aspect of the Abrahamic covenant (Gen. 12:2; 13:16; 15:5; 17:2,4-6,16; 22:17, 26:4,24; 28:3,14; 35:11) was now really gaining momentum. The God of Abraham, Isaac and Jacob would again demonstrate His faithfulness to His people.

Jacob lived in Canaan and Mesopotamia for 130 years (47:9) and in Egypt for 17 years (47:28). He had now reached his one hundred forty-seventh year, the year of his death. So he summoned Joseph and told him to take an oath: "Place now your hand under my thigh" (47:29). It was the same command that Abraham had given to his servant who was going out to search for a bride for Isaac (24:2). The action accompanied an especially solemn form of oath, with the hand of one person being placed near the organ of generation of another. In this case it was used because Jacob insisted on being buried not in Egypt but in Canaan, where his forefathers had been buried (47:29,30). In both cases, ties of family kinship were strongly emphasized (see 24:3,4). Abraham had wanted Isaac to be joined with his relatives in life; Jacob wanted to be joined with his relatives in death.

After Joseph had taken the oath, Jacob bowed down "at the head of the bed." The importance of his request and the energy he had expended in making it had apparently exhausted him (47:31).

Hebrews 11:21 quotes this passage, but it does so from the ancient Greek translation of the Old Testament, which reads "staff" instead of "bed" (the original Hebrew consonants of the word in question could be read either way, depending on the vowels that were pronounced along with them). So Hebrews 11:21 tells us that Jacob "worshiped, leaning on the top of his staff."

It is difficult to make a choice between the Genesis reading and the reading in Hebrews, because each has obvious merit. The Genesis 47:31 reading, "bed," fits in well contextually with 48:1,2. On the other hand, the Hebrews 11:21 reading, "staff," is not out of place there and would work equally well in Genesis 47:31. On balance, then, the reading "staff" is probably best for both passages.

Footnote

1. See especially J. Van Seters, *The Hyksos: A New Investigation* (New Haven: Yale University Press, 1966), pp. 127-151.

12

JACOB & JOSEPH:
Their Last Days
Genesis 48:1—50:26

The story of how a loving father and his favorite son lived out their final years concludes our study of the text of the book of Genesis.

Most of this three-chapter section details events that preceded Jacob's death. Only twelve verses are allotted to Joseph's last days.

The End of Jacob's Life—48:1—50:14

Jacob had already expressed his willingness to die, now that he had seen Joseph for the first time after a long separation and now that the whole family was together again (46:30).

But Jacob still needed to do a few things to put his house and affairs in order. For example, he needed to take care of bequeathing his estate to his heirs. In this case, bequeathal essentially amounted to pronouncing various blessings on Joseph's sons as well as on his own.

Blessing Joseph's Sons—48:1-22

As soon as Joseph was told that his father had become ill, he decided to take his two sons, Manasseh and Ephraim, and go to visit him (48:1). When they arrived at Jacob's house, Jacob exerted himself and sat up in bed (48:2). He then reminded Joseph of how God Almighty had appeared to him at Luz (later renamed Bethel) in Canaan and had renewed to him the twin promises of land and descendants (48:3,4; see 28:13,14 and especially 35:11,12).

By using the name "God Almighty," Jacob was acknowledging that only an all-powerful God could have made such far-reaching promises with the assurance that they would be fulfilled (see also 17:1,2; 28:3; 35:11; 43:14). And we are again reminded that "God Almighty" was the distinctive and characteristic name of God used by the patriarchs (Exod. 6:3).

Jacob now proceeded to adopt Joseph's two sons. Although Manasseh was Joseph's firstborn (Gen. 41:51), Jacob referred to the two boys as "Ephraim and Manasseh" (48:5). He spoke Ephraim's name first in anticipation of the fact that he would bless Ephraim first and Manasseh second (48:14-20).

Jacob went on to declare that Ephraim and Manasseh would now be his, just as Reuben and Simeon were his. In other words, Ephraim and Manasseh would enjoy equal status with Jacob's firstborn son (Reuben) and second son (Simeon; see 35:23). Although Jacob had 12 sons, Joseph's portion of Jacob's inheritance would be divided between Ephraim and Manasseh, making a total of 13 tribal allotments. To reduce the number back down to 12 again, the territorial share belonging to Levi (Jacob's third son; see 29:34; 35:23) would be eliminated. The Levites would be given only a number of towns with their surrounding pasture lands (Josh. 14:4).

Jacob's adoption of Ephraim and Manasseh would make it necessary for Joseph's next two sons to move up and take their places as far as Joseph's eventual bequeathal of his own estate was concerned. They in turn would perpetuate the names of Ephraim and Manasseh for inheritance purposes (Gen. 48:6).

Jacob's reminder to Joseph of his mother Rachel's untimely death on the way back from Paddan ("the plain"; the word is an abbreviation of *Paddan-aram;* see 25:20) as they approached

Bethlehem (48:7; see 35:16-19) was probably intended to justify Jacob's adoption of Ephraim and Manasseh. In effect, they took the place of other sons that Rachel might have been expected to bear if she had continued to live. By the same token Joseph, still young and virile, had plenty of time to father additional sons through one or more wives!

Apparently Jacob had not met Manasseh and Ephraim yet, so when Joseph brought them in Jacob wanted to know who they were (48:8). It is also possible, of course, that his question was due to the fact that he couldn't see them clearly because of poor vision (48:10). In any event, Joseph answered by saying that they were the sons that God had given him (48:9). Joseph used words that were beautifully reminiscent of Jacob's own words to Esau in response to a similar question years earlier (33:5). We, too, would do well to acknowledge our own children as gifts from a loving God whenever opportunity to do so presents itself.

Like Isaac in his old age (27:1), the elderly Jacob had weak eyes and was hardly able to see (48:10). So he asked Joseph to bring the boys closer to him in order that he could bless them. As they sat on Jacob's knees, he kissed and embraced them in an act probably symbolic of adoption procedures (48:10-12; see especially 30:3). Jacob was thrilled at having the opportunity of seeing not only Joseph but also Joseph's sons (48:11).

After Joseph had lifted the boys down from Jacob's knees and bowed low in respect before him (48:12), he placed Ephraim in front of Jacob's left hand and Manasseh in front of Jacob's right hand (48:13). This was to make sure that Jacob would put his right hand on the head of Manasseh, Joseph's firstborn, as he blessed Joseph's two sons. But Jacob, who had other plans, crossed his arms as he performed the blessing, putting his right hand on Ephraim's head and his left on Manasseh's (48:14).

Then Jacob blessed the boys. He invoked the name of God (48:15) in the person of the angel (48:16) who had earlier blessed Jacob himself (32:29). Jacob's blessing is beautiful in itself, depicting God as Companion, Shepherd and Redeemer. And as it was true of Jacob, so it is true of all believers: our God is with us, He leads us, He saves us.

Jacob also prayed that his own name and the names of Abraham and Isaac would be perpetuated in the names of

136

Ephraim and Manasseh. He further prayed that the boys would produce a multitude of descendants in the land (48:16). Although it may be tedious for us to repeat it by now, we must once again observe the reference to land and descendants, the two main aspects of the Abrahamic covenant.

Joseph was displeased when he saw his father's right hand on Ephraim's head, so he took hold of the hand in order to shift it over to Manasseh's head. But Jacob refused to move his hand. He indicated that although Manasseh would also be greatly blessed, nevertheless the younger son would be greater than the older (48:17-20).

Ephraim's descendants did become the most powerful tribe in the north during the time of the divided monarchy (931 to 722 B. C.). In fact, "Ephraim" was one of the names used by the prophets to refer to the northern kingdom (see, for example, Hosea 9:13; 12:1,8). Again we notice the tendency in Genesis (and throughout the Old Testament, for that matter) to bypass the firstborn in deference to a younger son. God wanted to make sure that His people were not unduly restricted by the tenacious legal custom known as primogeniture.

Jacob told Joseph that he was about to die but that God would be with Joseph and bring him back to Canaan, the land of his forefathers (48:21). Years later, Joseph would echo those words to his brothers just before his own death (50:24). At the same time, he would declare that they were to carry his bones back to Canaan with them (50:25). In such intricate ways the promises of a faithful God are transmitted from generation to generation!

Jacob also gave Joseph a preliminary gift before blessing all twelve brothers with blessings appropriate to each (49:28). Joseph was granted a mountain "ridge" or "shoulder" (48:22 NASB margin), the Hebrew word for which can also be read as the place-name *Shechem*. Since Joseph was later buried at Shechem in a plot of ground that became the property of his descendants (Josh. 24:32; see also Gen. 33:19; John 4:5), Shechem was probably the reference intended in Genesis 48:22.

Jacob said that he took the place from the Amorites in battle, a possible allusion to the plunder of Shechem by Jacob's sons (34:27-29). Needless to say, it could also be a reference to a battle otherwise unmentioned in the Old Testament.

Blessing Jacob's Sons—49:1-28

Genesis 49:2-27 is by far the longest poem in the book of Genesis. Often entitled "The Blessing of Jacob" by modern scholars, it is one of the oldest poems of any length in the entire Bible.[1] It is also one of a series of poetic blessings in Genesis that includes those of Noah (9:26,27), Melchizedek (14:19,20), Isaac (27:27-29; 27:39,40) and another by Jacob himself (48:15,16).

Because of its length, its complexity, its age and the fact that it is a poem, the Blessing of Jacob contains numerous rare words and unusual grammatical constructions. Such factors make it one of the most difficult chapters in Genesis to interpret in detail. In broad outline, however, its message and purpose are clear.

Shortly before his death, Jacob summoned his sons to gather around him. He wanted to tell them what was going to happen to them in the future (49:1). Not all of his prophecies would be fulfilled at the same time, of course. Some of the blessings turned out to be curses, while others are descriptions of character as well as predictions of future events.

After an introductory statement to set the stage and tone of the blessings (49:2), Jacob addressed each son individually, except for Simeon and Levi, who were two of a kind—birds of a feather, we would say! The order in which he addressed them was neither that of their birth (29:31–30:24) nor that of the listing in 35:23-26. These two listings and the Blessing of Jacob do, however, mention the first four sons in the order of their birth.

(1) *Reuben,* Jacob's firstborn, was initially described by Jacob as being supreme in honor and might because he was the firstfruits of Jacob's strength (49:3). But as we learned earlier, Reuben had cohabited with Bilhah, Jacob's concubine (35:22), perhaps even on more than one occasion. He seems to have been a man of impulse and indecision (see Judg. 5:15,16), as "uncontrolled as water" (Gen. 49:4). Because of his sinful activity, he would lose the supremacy due to him as the firstborn. His birthright would be given to Joseph's descendants (1 Chron. 5:1).

(2) *Simeon* and

(3) *Levi* were addressed together because they shared certain things in common: violence, anger, and fierceness (Gen. 49:5-7). As in the case of Reuben, Jacob's blessing turned into a curse (49:7) for Simeon and Levi because of their murder of the male

citizens of Shechem years before (34:25-31). Piling crime upon crime, they had also crippled the oxen belonging to Shechem by cutting the tendons in their legs (49:6).

Jacob stated poetically that he didn't want to associate with Simeon or Levi any longer (49:6). Then he indicated directly that their tribes would some day be dispersed and scattered throughout the other Israelite tribes (49:7).

And so it happened. Simeon became a part of Judah (Josh. 19:1,9), eventually losing its identity by being absorbed into it. The so-called "Blessing of Moses" (Deut. 33), another very ancient poem containing predictions about the characterizations of the twelve tribes of Israel, doesn't even mention Simeon!

As for Levi, his descendants received no extensive territory of their own, as we mentioned earlier. Forty-eight towns, together with the pasture lands surrounding them, were the Levites' only territorial inheritance (Josh. 14:4; 21:41,42; Num. 35:1-8), however honorable (Num. 18:21-24).

(4) The blessing on *Judah* (Gen. 49:8-12) rivals the one on Joseph (49:22-26) in length. Judah and Joseph would father the most powerful tribes in Israel and would compete for leadership in later generations, a fact reflected in 1 Chronicles 5:1,2.

Genesis 49:8 contains a double pun on Judah's name, since the Hebrew words for "praise" (see also 29:35) and "hand" resemble the word "Judah." The wording of 49:8 is also strongly reminiscent of Isaac's blessings on Jacob (see especially 27:29) and Esau (see especially 27:40), as well as of Joseph's memorable dreams (37:5-10).

The image of Judah (or Israel) as a lion (49:9) became common in later biblical literature (Num. 24:9; Micah 5:8; Ezek. 19:1-7). In Revelation 5:5, Jesus is called "the Lion that is from the tribe of Judah" in demonstration of His conquering majesty. And in the very next verse He is called the "Lamb" in demonstration of His meekness and His willingness to be sacrificed for the sins of the world (see also John 1:29).

Genesis 49:10 is undoubtedly the most well-known and best-loved verse in the Blessing of Jacob. Jewish and Christian interpreters alike have seen in it a prediction of the coming Messiah. It may well contain just such a prediction, although the verse is not easy to translate. But if it is indeed Messianic, the

New Testament ignored that fact since it nowhere quoted the verse in whole or in part.

The crux of the problem is the word traditionally rendered as "Shiloh." Elsewhere in the Old Testament, the place-name Shiloh is never spelled like it is in the Hebrew text of this verse, nor is "Shiloh" ever elsewhere a name for the Messiah. So other possibilities have been suggested, such as reading the crucial line as follows: "until he comes to whom it belongs" (*RSV;* see also Ezek. 21:27). That translation, however, requires an emendation of the Hebrew consonantal text.

Many recent scholars prefer to vocalize the Hebrew text slightly differently than the Jewish oral tradition did and to read the crucial line something like this: "until tribute comes to him" (see also Isa. 18:7). Such a reading forms an excellent parallel to the final line of the verse and results in the following translation for the verse as a whole:

> "The scepter shall not depart from Judah,
>   Nor the ruler's staff from between his feet,
>   Until tribute comes to him
>   And the people's obedience belongs to him."

This solution has the advantage of making good sense out of a difficult verse, and it also preserves the parallelism of successive lines so characteristic of Hebrew poetry in general and of this poem in particular.

Whether Messianic or not, Genesis 49:10 represents Judah's descendants as being powerful and conquering for generations on end. The scepter motif is reflected also in Numbers 24:17, another verse that has been traditionally considered Messianic. Like Genesis 49:10, however, it is never quoted or referred to in the New Testament.

Genesis 49:11,12 perhaps foresaw the time in the future when Judah would cease to be a wandering tribe and would settle down to a more established life. It also hints at the prosperity Judah would some day enjoy.

(5) The blessing on *Zebulun* (49:13) is perplexing, because his tribal territory (see Josh. 19:10-16) was landlocked by those of Asher and Manasseh. But it was close enough to the Mediterra-

nean to "draw out the abundance of the seas" (Deut. 33:19), that is, to participate in seaborne commerce. And maybe that's all Genesis 49:13 intended to say.

(6) *Issachar's* blessing contains a rare word, "sheepfolds" (49:14), that appears elsewhere only in Judges 5:16 and in a related form in Psalm 68:13. In all three cases it can also be translated either "saddlebags" or "campfires," and recent scholarship is divided as to its meaning.

Fortunately, the total thrust of the blessing is unaffected by this minor difficulty. Issachar, though sturdy and strong, would be pressed into doing forced labor for another tribe or nation (Gen. 49:14,15). For a possible fulfillment of this prophecy, see Judges 5:15.

(7) *Dan's* descendants would "judge" their people (or "rule" them; the word is a pun on the name "Dan"). They would take their rightful place among Israel's tribes (Gen. 49:16). Dan's characterization as a treacherous serpent (49:17) was entirely appropriate, as Judges 18:27 demonstrates.

Before proceeding to bless the rest of his sons, Jacob paused to catch his breath with the heartfelt prayer, "For Thy salvation I wait, O LORD" (Gen. 49:18). An elderly man on his deathbed, Jacob begged for God's help as he continued his strenuous speech, a speech that must have taxed all his physical, intellectual and spiritual faculties.

Such a plea was entirely in character when voiced by God's people (see, for example, Isa. 25:9). It can also serve us today as a beautiful model prayer, because it demonstrates one man's patience as well as his confidence in the Lord's love and concern for him.

(8) In *Gad's* brief blessing (Gen. 49:19), there are three puns on his name ("raiders" once and "raid" twice)! Located east of the Jordan river on the border of Moab (Josh. 13:24-28), the tribe of Gad was vulnerable to raids from its southern neighbor, as the ninth-century B.C. Mesha Stone illustrates.[2]

(9) *Asher's* coastal location (Josh. 19:24-31) and fertile farmlands would make them wealthy and enable them to produce delicacies fit for a king (Gen. 49:20).

(10) The characterization of *Naphtali* as a "doe let loose" (49:21) probably refers to the independent spirit of that tribe.

They were located in the hill country north of the Sea of Galilee (Josh. 19:32-39).

(11) Jacob's blessing on *Joseph* (Gen. 49:22-26) is about the same length as his blessing on Judah (49:8-12). It underscores the importance of the tribes that would some day descend from Joseph's sons, Manasseh and Ephraim. It also illustrates, however incidentally, Jacob's insistence that Ephraim should be more powerful than Manasseh (48:5,14-20) because it puns on Ephraim's name (the Hebrew word for "fruitful," used twice in 49:22, is similar to the word "Ephraim").

The tendency of Ephraim's descendants to expand their territory (49:22), their victories in battle (49:23,24), the fertility of their fields as God blessed their crops (49:25,26), and their supremacy over the other tribes, especially in the north (49:26)—all would be amply illustrated in Ephraim's later history (Josh. 16:5-10; 17:14-18; Judg. 8:1; 12:1; Isa. 7:1,2; Hos. 12:8; 13:1).

A striking feature of Joseph's blessing is the series of names by which Jacob referred to God (Gen. 49:24,25). He called Him "the Mighty One of Jacob" (see also Isa. 49:26), "the Shepherd" (see Gen. 48:15; Ps. 23:1), "the Stone of Israel" (see, for example, Ps. 18:2 and especially 19:14), "the God of [Joseph's] father" (see Gen. 31:29,42) and "the Almighty," the most characteristic patriarchal designation for God.

The series reminds us again how numerous God's qualities and attributes are. No matter how serious our problems might seem, He has infinite resources to help us. If we could only learn to take Him at His word and trust Him more completely!

(12) Among the descendants of Jacob's youngest son, *Benjamin,* were many who committed acts of lustfulness and savagery (see Judg. 19—21). So Jacob appropriately pictured Benjamin as a vicious wolf (Gen. 49:27).

The Blessing of Jacob closes with a statement that stresses the suitability of the blessing he gave each of his sons (49:28). Later developments proved his evaluation to be correct in every case, since God Himself was the ultimate source of Jacob's ability to foresee the future destiny of his sons and their descendants.

Jacob's Death and Burial—49:29—50:14

The book of Genesis now draws rapidly to a close. After Jacob had blessed his 12 sons, he told them that he was about to join his ancestors in death. He made his sons promise to bury him in the cave of Machpelah where the other patriarchs and their wives, as well as his own wife Leah (but not Rachel; see 35:19), had been buried (49:29-32). Having given his sons that final command, Jacob died (49:33) at the ripe old age of 147 years (47:28).

Joseph, who showed his emotions more openly than his brothers did (see 42:24; 43:30; 45:14,15; 46:29; 50:17), wept over his father (50:1). He then instructed the "physicians" to embalm Jacob (50:2). He may have deliberately avoided using the services of professional embalmers because of the accompanying pagan religious ceremonies such services would have entailed. The 40 days required for the embalming and the 70 days the Egyptians mourned for Jacob (50:3) may have overlapped, but in any event the time periods were in general harmony with what we know of ancient Egyptian custom.[3]

After the days of mourning were over, Joseph asked for and received the pharaoh's permission to take Jacob's body to Canaan for burial (50:4-6). A large number of people, including Jacob's household and many prominent Egyptians, made the trip (50:7-9). En route, they stopped at the threshing floor of Atad (a place of uncertain location) near the Jordan river. The stock Old Testament phrase, "beyond the Jordan," is sometimes used ambiguously. It can refer to either side of the river, and the context is not always clear enough to enable us to be sure which side is intended. In this case, however, the west side is most likely since Hebron, the destination of Jacob's mourners, is located west of the Jordan valley.

While at the threshing floor, the group held a seven-day ceremonial lamentation for Jacob. When the local Canaanite inhabitants observed it they renamed the place *Abel-mizraim*. The name means both "mourning of Egypt" and "meadow of Egypt," so the designation was a possible pun (50:10,11).

The mourners then continued on their way and buried Jacob in Hebron. Afterwards they all returned to Egypt (50:12-14).

The End of Joseph's Life—50:15-26

With Jacob now dead and buried, the last dozen verses of the book of Genesis describe Joseph's final days.

Joseph Reaffirms His Forgiveness—50:15-21

As soon as Joseph's brothers realized the full implications of Jacob's death, they became afraid that Joseph would now seek revenge against them for selling him as a slave (50:15). We remember that Esau had planned to take similar action against Jacob as soon as Isaac died (see 27:41).

So the brothers warned Joseph that Jacob had told them to plead for Joseph's forgiveness. Joseph wept when he received the message, perhaps partly because he felt that his brothers had falsely implicated Jacob in their story and was saddened by the lengths to which they would go to save themselves, perhaps partly at his own failure to have reassured them long before this (50:16,17). The brothers even offered to be Joseph's slaves (50:18), just as Judah had done earlier (44:33).

But Joseph assured the men that he would not play God by taking matters into his own hands (50:19). Indeed, he *couldn't* do so, any more than his father Jacob could have done so in other circumstances years before (30:2).

Joseph then gave his brothers an important lesson about the providence of God, who had planned everything that had happened so that only good would result. Genesis 50:20 is the Old Testament equivalent of Romans 8:28.

Joseph's generosity, his spirit of forgiveness, his loving concern again expressed themselves. He told his brothers once more not to be afraid (see Gen. 50:19,21). He also promised to provide them and their children with everything they needed.

What a beautiful illustration of our God, who calms our fears, assures us of His providence, and promises to supply all our needs "according to His riches in glory in Christ Jesus" (Phil. 4:19)!

Joseph's Death and Burial—50:22-26

Even after his father had died, Joseph continued to make his home in Egypt. He lived to the age of 110 years (Gen. 50:22,26) which, as we noted earlier in our study (see chap. 2), was considered to be the ideal lifespan, according to ancient Egyptian records.

Joseph had the privilege of seeing his son Ephraim's children down to the third generation (50:23), an experience similar to those enjoyed by other patriarchs (see, for example, Job 42:16). Joseph's firstborn, Manasseh, had a son named Machir, whose children were adopted by Joseph (Gen. 50:23; see 30:3; 48:10-12). Machir became the ancestor of a powerful nation (Josh. 17:1), and his name was used as a virtual synonym for "Manasseh" in Judges 5:14.

When the time came for Joseph to die, he told his brothers twice that God would "visit" them (Gen. 50:24,25 *NASB* margin). The verb "visit" means "take care of, pay special attention to" when used in contexts like this one. The Lord would not forget His promises to Abraham, to Isaac, to Jacob or to their descendants. He would continue to express His loving concern for the people of Israel and would bring them back to Canaan.

And Joseph, of course, wanted to make that memorable trip too. So he made his brothers promise to carry his bones along with them (50:25). They couldn't fulfill their promise, however, because by the time of that trip (called "the exodus"; see Heb. 11:22) they, too, had long since died. But their descendants were able to keep the promise (Exod. 13:19), and when they arrived in Canaan they lovingly buried Joseph's remains at Shechem, on the plot of ground that Jacob had purchased from Hamor's sons (Josh. 24:32; see Gen. 33:19).

After his brothers had taken the oath that Joseph requested, he died, was embalmed and was placed in a sarcophagus. To all intents and purposes, the last of the patriarchs had now passed from the scene, and our story, in one sense, is over. The book of Genesis, the book that began with creation and life, concluded with old age and death. It started "in the beginning" (1:1) and ended "in a coffin in Egypt" (50:26).

If that coffin had been the final curtain in the biblical drama, we would be of all people most miserable. But it wasn't, of course! If we wanted to, we could simply turn the page and begin reading the book of Exodus—Act Two in the exciting account of how God continued to fulfill the twin patriarchal promises of descendants and homeland.

But that, after all, is another story.

Footnotes

1. See, for example, W. F. Albright, *Yahweh and the Gods of Canaan* (Garden City: Doubleday & Company, Inc., 1968), pp. 19, 20.

2. See Albright in J. B. Pritchard, editor, *Ancient Near Eastern Texts*, second edition (Princeton: Princeton University Press, 1955), p. 320.

3. See J. J. Davis. *Mummies, Men and Madness* (Winona Lake: BMH Books, 1972), pp. 97-100.

13

THE PATRIARCHS:
Though Dead, They Speak

The eleventh chapter of Hebrews is often referred to as "the roll call of the faithful." The chapter as a whole contains 40 verses and is well worth reading many times over. In cameo-like portraits, it depicts the essential characteristics and activities that made it possible for certain people from the pages of the Old Testament to qualify for a place in a list of men and women who displayed unusually great faith.

The heart of the chapter is 11:4-32, a section that gets down to specific cases and actually names a number of people whose lives exemplified genuine faith in God. It is to the credit of the patriarchs that of those 29 verses more than half—15, to be exact—are devoted to detailing the ways in which the patriarchs and their wives proved themselves to be men and women of faith (11: 8-22).

It is said of Abel, the first person to be mentioned in the main section (11:4-32), that, because of his faith, "though he is dead, he still speaks" (11:4). The same could be said of the patriarchs as well. They all died, but through their faith they still speak to us today.

They give us, in fact, a kind of patriarchal theology. It is not laid out in orderly and systematic fashion, to be sure. But it is nonetheless helpful for all that. The patriarchal narratives in Genesis 11:27–50:26 give us a wealth of practical information about God's relationship to man, man's relationship to God and man's relationship to man.

Our final study in this book will concentrate on several aspects of each of these three very important subjects.

What the Patriarchs Tell Us
About God's Relationship to Man

We understand the word "man" here, of course, in its generic sense, meaning "men, women, boys and girls." The story of the patriarchs is an exciting and absorbing account about actual people in actual situations.

Needless to say, however, the real hero of the patriarchal narratives is God Himself (as we noted at the beginning of chap. 2). Even when He does not occupy center stage in the story, He is at least nearby, waiting to relate Himself to His people in one way or other. In fact, He is eager to come to the aid of all who need Him. The God of the patriarchs is our God as well, the God who seeks, the God who acts.[1]

He takes the initiative in acting on behalf of His people. Even when we are not particularly looking for Him or aware of His presence, He is there. He reveals Himself to us in various ways—in nature, through conscience, in His Word, through the witness of the Holy Spirit in our lives, and so forth. And He revealed Himself to the patriarchs in various ways as well: in dreams (Gen. 28:12-17), in visions (15:1), in the person of the angel of the Lord (22:11).[2]

God also made Himself known to the patriarchs in a way more difficult to define even than these. We are told often that He "appeared" to them (17:1, for example). That verb means, literally, that God "allowed Himself to be seen" by the patriarchs. This does not imply that they saw Him in all the fullness of His splendor and glory, but rather that they experienced His spiritual presence in an intimate and personal way. They enjoyed communion and fellowship with Him to an exceptional degree.

The names that God gave to Himself or by which He allowed Himself to be called are another indication of His willingness to disclose His plans and purposes to the patriarchs.

El Elyon was a name by which both Abraham and Melchizedek referred to God (14:18-20,22). It means "God Most High" and stresses the fact that the one true God is God *par excellence,* that He occupies the supreme position in the universe over all other so-called "gods," whether real or imagined. In that same context where Abraham and Melchizedek appear together God is also called "Creator of heaven and earth" (14:19,22 *NASB* margin; see also 24:3), a name emphasizing the fact that everything that is owes its origin and continued existence to Him.

El Shaddai (see, for example, 17:1) was the divine name most characteristic of the patriarchal period (Exod. 6:3). While its literal meaning was probably something like "God, the Mountain One," for all practical purposes the traditional translation, "God Almighty," gets at the functional significance of the name. "God Almighty" was a designation that stressed the omnipotence of God in the lives of the patriarchs. God Almighty, because He is all-powerful, had the power to help them overcome all their difficulties. He was able to protect them when they were traveling (even in foreign countries), to supply them with all the food and clothing and shelter they needed (even to make them wealthy), to help them produce children (even when they were beyond the age of childbearing) and to give them success in whatever they attempted to do (even when naiveté and superstition were their only native resources). In short, God Almighty (see also the name, "the Mighty One of Jacob," in Gen. 49:24) was the God whose strength was made perfect in their weakness (see 2 Cor. 12:9).

God is also the "Judge" of the whole earth (Gen. 18:25). He dealt with the patriarchs and deals with us in perfect justice. He destroyed Sodom, Gomorrah and the other towns in the plain because their inhabitants were sinful beyond recall, but at the same time "He rescued righteous Lot" (2 Pet. 2:7) "out of the midst of the overthrow" (Gen. 19:29). As the Judge of us all, God is eminently able to distinguish between His own children and the children of Satan. His holiness often saves, but it also sears.

El Olam (21:33), another name by which God was known during the patriarchal period, means "God Everlasting" and stresses His eternal nature. Implicit in the name is continuity, the fact that although our lives are brief at best God has always existed and always will exist. He and His promises are dependable. They continue on from generation to generation, because time is for Him not an obstacle but an opportunity. Jacob, in referring to "the God of my father" (31:5,42), could do so with the confidence that the God who had been Isaac's God and Abraham's God would also be his own God and his children's God and their children's God throughout endless ages!

"The fear of Isaac" (31:42; see also 31:53) is a phrase that is doubtless another title for the God of the patriarchs. If correctly translated, it highlights the fact that God wants His people to worship Him, to respect Him, to honor Him, to hold Him in awe. It emphasizes, in other words, God's transcendence, His aloofness, His otherness, His distance from us. But if as some modern scholars contend it means "the Kinsman of Isaac," it emphasizes God's immanence, His cordiality, His similarity to us, His nearness to us.

How can God be both far away and close at hand at the same time? His omnipresence (as it has traditionally been called) is certainly one of the mysteries of His being. I plan to ask Him for a detailed explanation when I get to heaven! But in the meantime I must be content with observing that the Bible teaches both His distance and His nearness. Indeed, there is a beautiful statement of both in Isaiah 57:15, the first three lines of which focus on God's transcendence and the last three on His immanence:

> "For thus says the high and exalted One
> Who lives forever, whose name is Holy,
> 'I dwell on a high and holy place,
> And also with the contrite and lowly of spirit
> In order to revive the spirit of the lowly
> And to revive the heart of the contrite.' "

Two final names of God that were used during the patriarchal period and that deserve special mention are "the Shepherd" and "the Stone of Israel" (Gen. 49:24). Both are found in the same line of the same verse, even though they appear at first blush to be unrelated to each other.

Closer examination, however, reveals that both names have to do with God as Protector of His people. Like a shepherd, our God watches over us, expresses His concern for us, and cares for our needs. Like a fortress made of stone and rock, our God shields (see 15:1) us from the onslaughts of Satan and shelters us from the storms and stresses of life that threaten to overwhelm us. He gives us the assurance that our problems and difficulties don't have to defeat us, whether in the symbolism of lambs protected by the strong arm of a shepherd or of birds protected in the crevice of a rocky cliff.

The patriarchs must have learned a great deal about the nature of their God just by thinking through the implications of His many names!

But God's relationship to them was expressed in countless other ways as well. His continuing concern for them was a reflection of other attributes of His that we haven't mentioned in this chapter. Let's look at a few of them.

Every time God told one of the patriarchs about something that was going to happen in the future, He was giving tangible expression to His omniscience. Only a God who knows everything dares to make such far-ranging and far-reaching predictions.

Every time God confirmed His covenant with the patriarchs, He was expressing His love and faithfulness to them and their descendants. Covenants were not entered into lightly in ancient times, and God seemed to derive special delight from taking oaths in His own name (22:16; see Heb. 6:13).

Every time God made one of the patriarchs wealthy or successful, He was demonstrating His providence in a special way. He was reminding them that all they could ever hope to be or have depended on His goodness and grace.

Every time God rescued the patriarchs from danger, He showed them that He was merciful (see especially Gen. 19:16). And His mercies are without limitation; as Lamentations 3:23 puts it, "they are new every morning."

Every time God—but perhaps we've already given enough

examples. We could comment on His sovereignty, His elective purpose, His patience, His incredible willingness to bless and strengthen and give to people who were often unwilling to bless and strengthen and give in return.

Although for the patriarchs Calvary could have been only the dimmest of hopes almost 2000 years in the future, their God maintained a warm and cordial relationship indeed toward them. The more spiritually perceptive among them must have been supremely grateful for the depth of that relationship.

Shouldn't we, who live almost 2000 years after Calvary, be infinitely more grateful for the additional blessings God has showered down on us through our Lord Jesus Christ?

What the Patriarchs Tell Us
About Man's Relationship to God

Relationship is always a two-way street. As God related Himself to the patriarchs in various ways, so also they related themselves to Him in various ways.

It has become a commonplace in our time to assert that Moses was the first Old Testament figure to embrace monotheism, the belief that there is only one God.[3] Theoretical monotheism has been observed by recent scholars in such passages as Deuteronomy 4:35,39; 6:4; and 32:39. But it should be pointed out that the ancient Hebrew people tended to be short on theory and long on practice. They were not theologians or philosophers so much as servants and worshipers. Moses as well was much more a practical monotheist than a theoretical monotheist.

And the same evaluation applies to the patriarchs. In their better moments, they loved the Lord with all their hearts and souls and minds and strength. Although their ancestors had been polytheists (Josh. 24:2), there were times of deep spiritual significance in their own lives when they got rid of the other gods, real or imagined, that they had been accustomed to worshiping (Gen. 35:2-4). At such times, the one true God so monopolized their attention and experience that they had no time or opportunity for other loyalties. The patriarchs were practical monotheists, so God was able to slowly, surely and firmly wean them away from the worship of all that was unworthy. And they learned to love Him for it!

The means that God used to assure that the patriarchs would give Him their undivided loyalty was the covenant. By its very nature, entering into a covenant tends toward an exclusive relationship that brooks no rivals. "I will be their God, and they shall be My people" (Jer. 31:33; see also Gen. 17:7) became a characteristic phrase throughout the Old Testament expressing the covenant relationship. As the ancient Israelites were to worship God alone because of their covenant relationship to Him, so also the true Christian is to refer only to Jesus Christ as "Lord" (Rom. 10:9).

The Abrahamic covenant was solemnized by sacrifice, the slaughter and offering of animals to the Lord (Gen. 15:9,10). The patriarchs often built altars at places where they had significant spiritual experiences. The best known of these is doubtless the one at Moriah, where the two basic principles of Old Testament sacrifice were beautifully exemplified: sacrifice as the gift of life (Isaac) to God, and sacrifice as the substitution of life (the ram; see 22:9-13).

The mention of sacrifice helps us to recall the importance of the shedding of blood to pave the way for man's proper relationship to God throughout the Bible. "The life of the flesh is in the blood," and "it is the blood by reason of the life that makes atonement" (Lev. 17:11). The principle that shedding blood was a prerequisite for the removal of sin is not clearly expressed in the patriarchal narratives. But circumcision as the sign of the Abrahamic covenant reminds us, at the very least, that a general covenant becomes individually effective only as the individual relates himself in a personal way to a ceremony involving the shedding of blood.

That principle is important for us as well. We can become members of the covenant people of God only by confessing that "Christ died for our sins according to the Scriptures" (1 Cor. 15:3) and that "the blood of Jesus," God's Son, "cleanses us from all sin" (1 John 1:7).

Believing in God's covenant provisions for them made it possible for the patriarchs to enjoy communion and fellowship with Him. Over and over again, the Lord promised to be with them wherever they went, as we have already observed.

The constant presence of God in their lives might well have

had the effect of teaching them that their God was the God of other people and nations also. The patriarchs do not seem to have been conscious of that fact to the extent that they were overcome by a strong zeal to witness to their faith in the one true God, with the possible exception of the Abraham-Melchizedek encounter. But opportunities and incentive to witness to people of other nations were there for those who had the eyes to see them.

Canaan, after all, was the crossroads of the ancient world, and providentially so. People from the surrounding nations often had to travel through Canaan while going from one place to another. Separated from their own temples and priests by long distances, they could have become prime objects of witness on the part of the patriarchs and their descendants. Had the patriarchs been more zealous in buying up the opportunities, one aspect of God's call to Abraham would have begun to be fulfilled even in those early days: "In you all the families of the earth shall be blessed" (Gen. 12:3). Universal faith in the one true God would have been well on its way!

But while the faith of the patriarchs may not have been mission-minded, it was nonetheless fervent. They worshiped the Lord in numerous ways, and did so openly and unashamedly. They made promises and vows of various kinds to Him (see 28:20-22). They prayed long and loudly and often to Him, giving us enviable examples of persistence in the process (18:22-33; 32:26). They paid tithes to Him or to His representatives in gratitude for His goodness (14:20; 28:22). In short, they expressed their love to God in every way that was available to them.

This is not to say that the patriarchs were perfect either in their worship or their conduct, of course. One of the commendable qualities of Scripture that make it so eminently readable is that it does not gloss over the sins and frailties of even its greatest heroes. In the case of the patriarchs, the Bible presents them to us as they really were, warts and all!

It's not necessary for us to dwell again on the sins of violence, deceit, murder, rape, theft, etc., etc., that they committed. We have already commented on them at length. We simply observe once again that the patriarchs were real live people with real problems and that they committed real sins that were really judged by the living God. The patriarchs were tempted in all points just as we are and they often succumbed.

But their failures are not what the New Testament writers remembered them for. They were recalled, fondly and frequently, for their deep and abiding relationships to God, the most important of which was their faith that God could do the impossible. When they were closest to the center of His will, the quality of their faith was such that it could be compared favorably with our faith in the resurrection of Christ (Rom. 4:19-25).

And as the New Testament writers remembered the patriarchs most often for their faith in God, so also should we.

What the Patriarchs Tell us About Man's Relationship to Man

But "faith without works is dead" (Jas. 2:26). Dependence on God must be coupled with the willingness to act on that dependence if its genuineness is to be proven.

Some well-meaning activity is the outgrowth of sin rather than of faith, of course. When Sarah suggested to Abraham that it might be a good idea for him to cohabit with Hagar in order to produce a son who would fulfill God's promise, that was an example of sinful impatience rather than of confident faith. And when Abraham agreed to Sarah's proposal, that was an example of carnal weakness rather than of patient dependence on God and His promises.

Such examples, however, are of value to us only in showing us what *not* to do in analogous situations. The patriarchs have much to teach us positively in the complex matter of our relationships with other people, whether inside or outside the household of faith.

J. Strahan, in his classic treatment of the beliefs, feelings, and aspirations of the patriarchs,[4] spends considerable time in discussing the moral and ethical standards to which they adhered, some of which were part and parcel of their culture and others of which were the direct result of their personal relationship to a loving God. We can learn much, even today, from the positive ideals that the patriarchs tried to emulate in their own lives.

The prompt courtesy that the patriarchs showed to their guests is a noteworthy characteristic that recurs again and again throughout the narratives (Gen. 18:2-7; 19:1-3; 24:28-32; 29:12, 13). The hospitality they provided for their visitors made them feel right at home. They seemed to take special delight in entertaining them as lavishly as their resources would allow.

Patriarchal generosity was expressed in other ways as well. A particularly fine example is to be found in Abraham's offer to Lot (13:9). In effect, Abraham told Lot that he could make use of whatever section of the Jordan valley region he desired, and that Abraham would content himself with what was left.

Springing from Abraham's generosity was also a commendable spirit of self-sacrifice. Risking life and limb, he dashed off to the north country to rescue his ungrateful nephew Lot from a band of marauding kings. Then, after saving Lot and his friends and after retrieving the plunder the kings had taken, he refused to keep any of the plunder for himself (14:14-16,21-24).

Strong ties of blood kinship developed in the patriarchs a sense of loyalty to each other, another quality demonstrated in Genesis 14. Such loyalty can be seen throughout the book of Genesis, especially in the many descriptions of patriarchal marriages that took place within the tribe or clan.

Times of joy and laughter, though not mentioned frequently in the patriarchal accounts, must have occurred often in their experience. They had a great deal to be thankful for and happy about, as passages such as 21:6 and 31:27 imply. Sharing joy always doubles it, and the patriarchs doubtless had many opportunities to prove that fact.

But while they knew how to laugh with each other, they also knew how to weep with each other. Like their later countrymen, they knew that "there is a time for every event under heaven— . . . a time to weep, and a time to laugh" (Eccles. 3:1,4). In fact, the patriarchs, along with other people in the ancient Near East, developed mourning and grieving into a fine art. When calamity or death struck, they tore their clothes (Gen. 37:29), dressed themselves in sackcloth (37:34), and wept uncontrollably, often for many days (37:34; 50:3,10).

In fact, the display of emotion, whether laughter or weeping or anger or any one of a number of others, still tends to be much more demonstrative and open in Eastern countries than in the

West. We have already noted how often Joseph wept as first his 10 older brothers, then Benjamin and finally Jacob arrived in Egypt, a series of events that reunited the whole family. And the account of that gradual reunion stresses Joseph's difficulty in controlling his emotions (42:24; 43:30,31; 45:1).

As laughter can be evoked by ties of kinship, so also can weeping. Jacob and Esau wept as they saw each other for the first time after long years of separation (33:4). The tears were probably a mixture of joy and remorse, but they strengthened the ties of brotherhood that had been strained to the breaking point. Esau, in fact, insisted on calling Jacob his "brother" on that occasion (33:9). Jacob had wronged Esau, but never mind—they were still brothers. Similarly, Joseph's brothers had wronged him, but never mind, said Joseph: "I am your brother" (45:4)!

In these incidents, we see something of the spirit of forgiveness that also characterized the patriarchs during moments of high moral and ethical sensitivity. Another example that comes readily to mind occurred near the end of Joseph's life. A touching scene full of forgiveness and selflessness unfolds before our eyes in 50:15-21. Joseph tells his brothers that even their crimes against him found their place in the perfect will of a God who never makes mistakes. They had sold Joseph into slavery in Egypt in order that God might use him to eventually save the whole family. Joseph's compassion and his depth of spiritual understanding on that occasion would be hard to parallel elsewhere in Scripture.

The patriarchs, being dead, yet speak. Like Joseph, they sob with rejoicing when most of us would scream with rage. Like Abraham, they rush to do God's will while most of us rationalize or refuse to do what we know He desires. And like Jacob, they love deeply and with infinite patience (29:20) while our love tends to be shallow and perfunctory. Although not perfect by any means, the lives of the patriarchs frequently put ours to shame by comparison.

But then why shouldn't they? After all, they were part of an unusually enlightened age, even though they lived long before the time of Moses or Paul or Jesus Christ. . . .

Footnotes

1. For a careful treatment of the theme of God in action see G. E. Wright, *God Who Acts* (London: SCM Press Ltd., 1952).

2. See especially G. Vos, *Biblical Theology* (Grand Rapids: Wm. B. Eerdmans Publishing Company, 1948), pp. 82-89.

3. See, for example, W. F. Albright, *From the Stone Age to Christianity*, second edition (Baltimore: The Johns Hopkins Press, 1957), pp. 271, 272.

4. J. Strahan, *Hebrew Ideals*, fourth edition (Edinburgh: T. & T. Clark, 1922).

BIBLIOGRAPHY

(Inclusion of a book in the following list does not necessarily indicate wholesale approval of the author's viewpoint or methodology.)

Aharoni, Yohanan, and Avi-Yonah, Michael. *The Macmillan Bible Atlas.* New York, New York: The Macmillan Company, 1968.

Albright, William F. *Archaeology and the Religion of Israel,* fourth edition. Baltimore, Maryland: The Johns Hopkins Press, 1956.

_____. *From the Stone Age to Christianity,* second edition. Baltimore, Maryland: The Johns Hopkins Press, 1957.

_____. *Yahweh and the Gods of Canaan.* Garden City, New York: Doubleday & Company, Inc., 1968.

Douglas, J. D., editor. *The New Bible Dictionary.* Grand Rapids, Michigan: Wm. B. Eerdmans Publishing Co., 1962.

Gaubert, Henri. *Abraham, Loved by God,* translated by Lancelot Sheppard. New York, New York: Hastings House, Publishers, 1968.

Kidner, Derek. *Genesis.* Downers Grove, Illinois: Inter-Varsity Press, 1967.

Kitchen, K. A. *Ancient Orient and Old Testament*. Chicago, Illinois: Inter-Varsity Press, 1966.

Lowenthal, Eric I. *The Joseph Narrative in Genesis*. New York, New York: Ktav Publishing House, Inc., 1973.

Pfeiffer, Charles F., editor. *The Biblical World*. Grand Rapids, Michigan: Baker Book House, 1966.

_____. *The Patriarchal Age*. Grand Rapids, Michigan: Baker Book House, 1961.

Pritchard, James B., editor. *Ancient Near Eastern Texts Relating to the Old Testament*, second edition. Princeton, New Jersey: Princeton University Press, 1955.

Sarna, Nahum M. *Understanding Genesis*. New York, New York: Schocken Books, 1966.

Speiser, E. A. *Genesis*. Garden City, New York: Doubleday & Company, Inc., 1964.

Strahan, James. *Hebrew Ideals*, fourth edition. Edinburgh, Scotland: T. & T. Clark, 1922.

Thompson, J. A. *The Bible and Archaeology*, revised edition. Grand Rapids, Michigan: Wm. B. Eerdmans Publishing Co., 1972.

Vos., Geerhardus. *Biblical Theology*. Grand Rapids, Michigan: Wm. B. Eerdmans Publishing Co., 1948.

Youngblood, Ronald. *The Heart of the Old Testament*. Grand Rapids, Michigan: Baker Book House, 1971.